HUMAN EXISTENCE
AND TRANSCENDENCE

THRESHOLDS IN PHILOSOPHY AND THEOLOGY

Jeffrey Bloechl and Kevin Hart, series editors

Philosophy is provoked and enriched by the claims of faith
in a revealed God. Theology is stimulated by its contact with
the philosophy that proposes to investigate the full range of
human experience. At the threshold where they meet, there
inevitably arises a discipline of reciprocal interrogation and
the promise of mutual enhancement. The works in this series
contribute to that discipline and that promise.

HUMAN EXISTENCE

AND TRANSCENDENCE

JEAN WAHL

TRANSLATED AND EDITED BY WILLIAM C. HACKETT
WITH JEFFREY HANSON

FOREWORD BY KEVIN HART

University of Notre Dame Press
Notre Dame, Indiana

University of Notre Dame Press
Notre Dame, Indiana 46556
www.undpress.nd.edu
All Rights Reserved

English Language Edition Copyright © 2016 by the University of Notre Dame

Translated by William C. Hackett from Jean Wahl, *Existence Humaine et Transcendance*, published by Éditions de la Baconnière – Neuchâtel, June 6, 1944. © Éditions de la Baconnière.

Published in the United States of America

Library of Congress Cataloging-in-Publication Data

Names: Wahl, Jean André, 1888-1974, author.
Title: Human existence and transcendence / Jean Wahl ; translated and edited by William C. Hackett, with Jeffrey Hanson ; foreword by Kevin Hart.
Other titles: Existence humaine et transcendence. English
Description: Notre Dame : University of Notre Dame Press, 2016. |
Series: Thresholds in philosophy and theology |
Includes bibliographical references and index.
Identifiers: LCCN 2016032983 (print) | LCCN 2016034178 (ebook) |
ISBN 9780268101060 (hardcover : alk. paper) |
ISBN 026810106X (hardcover : alk. paper) |
ISBN 9780268101084 (pdf) | ISBN 9780268101091 (epub)
Subjects: LCSH: Transcendence (Philosophy) | Ontology.
Classification: LCC BD362 .W3313 2016 (print) |
LCC BD362 (ebook) | DDC 111—dc23
LC record available at https://lccn.loc.gov/2016032983

Les circonstances ont empêché l'auteur de revoir les épreuves du présent ouvrage. L'éditeur s'excuse donc des erreurs qui pourraient ne pas avoir été corrigées et des initiatives qu'il a dû prendre sans l'agrément de l'auteur.

Circumstances prevented the author from reviewing the proofs of the present work. The publisher thereby apologizes for mistakes that may not have been corrected and initiatives that had to be undertaken without the agreement of the author.

[Editorial apology affixed to the beginning of the original French text, published June 1944]

CONTENTS

FOREWORD

Jean Wahl's *Human Existence and Transcendence* is a very important yet almost completely forgotten work in the history of twentieth-century French philosophy. It arose from a lecture given in 1937 and was expanded into a short book in the troubled years that followed. Apart from its intrinsic interest as a discussion of being, the absolute, and transcendence, the work is valuable insofar as it became a focal point for a great many European intellectuals. Their responses to Wahl's thoughts, especially on transcendence, at once clarify many issues to do with existentialism as well as hint how it was to be transformed by a later thinker such as Emmanuel Levinas (whom we see here as a young man in full flush of enthusiasm for Heidegger).

Is transcendence exclusively a theological notion, or can it be put to philosophical use? This is Wahl's animating question, and the question that excited or upset those who heard his lecture and the others who responded to it by mail. Wahl answers his own question: transcendence can indeed be lifted from the matrix of theology, reset as a concept, and then used to clarify the human situation. Of course, he was not the first or the only person to move in this direction. Heidegger had already rethought transcendence in *Sein und Zeit* (1927), having brooded on the concept's roots in the medieval tradition of the transcendentals: being, beauty, goodness, truth, and unity. Such things do not themselves settle into the Aristotelian categories but are found in all of them; they cross (*trans*) from one category to another. Centuries later in the *Critique of Pure Reason* (1781; 1787) Kant redirected this tradition, distinguishing between the transcendental and the transcendent. The former give conditions of possibility for knowledge; the latter exceed all possible knowledge. So Kant gives only a negative sense of transcendence. It is Heidegger who gives it a positive sense, which is human *Dasein*'s openness to pass from beings to being. This is fundamental-ontological transcendence, and it is this radical understanding of the concept that Levinas wishes to impress on Wahl in his letter to him after the lecture had been given.

In his letter Levinas points out that in rethinking transcendence Heidegger breaks decisively with theology. Here theology is regarded as limited by ontic concerns; one desires to pass from this world to another world above or beyond it, though this second world doubtless resembles ours in many ways (hell, purgatory, and heaven as evoked in Dante's *Commedia*, for example). Wahl is not entirely at ease with Levinas's response to his lecture, and he could well point out that his rethinking of transcendence as transascendence also overcomes a naïve theology: one transcends without term; there is no fall back into the immanence of a higher place. He also could remind Levinas of transcendence's other dimension, transdescendence, in which one is taken without term down into the depths. In later years Levinas will gladly learn from Wahl: *Totalité et infini* (1961) could not have been conceived without the transascendence of the other person, and much that Levinas fears is perhaps contained in the thought of transdescendence.[1] If transascendence is coordinate with the holy (and hence the ethical), its negative counterpart converges with the sacred.[2] Wahl himself cites D. H. Lawrence—he may well have *The Plumed Serpent* (1926) in mind—as a witness to the transdescendent.

Not that Wahl's rethinking of transcendence is limited to the uses to which Levinas finally put it. His distinction illuminates a whole tendency of modern European thought, the quest to explain phenomena by way of what preconditions them, whether that be by way of preexistent constitution (Fink), the neutral (Blanchot), or *la différance* (Derrida). Perhaps one could extend the explanatory power of transdescendence further back into the history of philosophy, from the critical philosophy to structuralism, but let us not try to press too hard on it. Already, with Levinas, Blanchot, and Derrida, it has done a job of work, as has its correlative idea, transcendence, which also quickens all three in their understanding of ethics. The work of transascendence is not yet over, and ironically it may well be the theologian's task, rather than the philosopher's, to continue it. For despite the power of various caricatures, in which Heidegger and Levinas both indulged themselves, Christian theology has never been committed to transcendence in the limited sense of passing from one world to another. The radical rethinking of God as infinite, as proposed by Saint Gregory of Nyssa in his argument with Eunomius, yields a massive elaboration of the Pauline figure in Philippians 3:13 of reaching forward to what is before him (δὲ ἔμπροσθεν ἐπεκτεινόμενος). For Gregory, the Christian life is continual transcendence of self into the abundant life of God. In this life, we do not believe *in* God so much as believe ourselves *into* God. And so it will be throughout eternity, though no longer in the mode of belief. One fruit of Wahl's famous lecture may well be to return the Christian to the most powerful contemporary advocate of Nicene orthodoxy and the boldest of the Cappadocian theologians. For Gregory's insistence on the metaphysical infinity of the divine shored up not only the divinity of Christ, which Eunomius had called into question, but also allowed for a better theological grasp of God as triune and stressed the importance of the apophatic strain in theology.

Let us return to Wahl. He was a considerable figure in midcentury French intellectual life, and indeed in Franco-American intellectual life. He was fluent in English, and lived for some years in the United States, setting up the discussions among writers and intellectuals known as Pontigny-en-Amérique. In that context he became acquainted with Wallace Stevens. In September 1942 Alfred A. Knopf published the great poet's *Parts of a World*, and then, a month later, Cummington Press produced a limited edition of a memorable work in that collection, "Notes toward a Supreme Fiction." Wahl wrote to Stevens's friend Henry Church after reading "Notes" and told him of the pleasure he had gained from reading it. Stevens later said to Church, "To give pleasure to an intelligent man, by this sort of thing, is as much as one can expect; and certainly I am most *content*, in the French sense of that word, to have pleased Jean Wahl."[3] More, Stevens appreciated Wahl's insight that in order to articulate a supreme fiction one must first strip away all other fictions.[4] It is pleasant to imagine Wahl, who was a professor at the Sorbonne (albeit not from 1942 to 1945, when he was mostly at Mount Holyoke College in South Hadley,

Massachusetts), reading some lines that come almost at the end of that magnificent poem:

> They will get it straight one day at the Sorbonne.
> We shall return at twilight from the lecture
> Pleased that the irrational is rational.[5]

Those who went home after Wahl's famous lecture might not have been convinced that the irrational is rational, which in any case was hardly what the lecturer wanted to show, but they were doubtless moved by the prospect of a style of transcendence that was entirely appropriate to human life as it is lived in the streets of Paris, South Hadley, and Hartford, Connecticut.

Wahl had significant, if subterranean, influences on generations of French and American people. He founded the Collège philosophique in Paris in 1945, notable for many events, not the least of which was a paper given on March 4, 1963, by Jacques Derrida which upset his former teacher Michel Foucault and led to a rift between them, the effects of which are still being felt in some quarters of the academy.[6] It was Wahl who indirectly taught American professors and their students about French existentialism and, more generally, about the philosophy of existence. Two generations of Americans read Sartre and others through lenses ground by Wahl. If his *A Short History of Existentialism* (1949) and *Philosophies of Existence* (1968) have largely served their purposes, a new generation of Americans with different concerns perhaps still needs to read Wahl's more enduring works, including Études kierkegaardiennes (1938), *Le malheur de la conscience dans la philosophie de Hegel* (1929), and of course *Existence humaine et transcendance* (1944).

We now have that last title available in English. So at last Anglophone readers can see an important text in the history of the vicissitudes of transcendence in the twentieth century, both in relation to philosophy and to theology. The book itself is an unusual one; in some ways, as Chris Hackett says in his introduction, it recalls Pascal's *Pensées*. All the more reason, then, for it to have a long historical introduction. The editor nicely leads the reader into Wahl's world, and indicates, with all due lightness, moments when our world unknowingly intersects with it and other moments when we could profit from knowing it better than we do. He and Jeffrey Hanson have done a fine job of rendering a host of European voices into English. This is an event that allows us to savor a precious moment in French intellectual life and to ponder its many consequences.

Kevin Hart
University of Virginia

NOTES

1. See Emmanuel Levinas, *Totality and Infinity: An Essay on Exteriority*, trans. Alphonso Lingis (The Hague: Martinus Nijhoff, 1979), 35n.

2. See Levinas, "Desacralization and Disenchantment," *Nine Talmudic Readings*, trans. and intro. Annette Aronowicz (Bloomington: Indiana University Press, 1990), 136–60.

3. Wallace Stevens to Henry Church, *Letters of Wallace Stevens*, ed. Holly Stevens (New York: Alfred A. Knopf, 1972), 430.

4. See Stevens, *Letters*, 431.

5. Wallace Stevens, *Collected Poetry and Prose*, ed. Frank Kermode and Joan Richardson (New York: Library of America, 1997), 351.

6. See Jacques Derrida, "Cogito and the History of Madness," *Writing and Difference*, trans. Alan Bass (London: Routledge and Kegan Paul, 1978), 31–63.

Introduction

Jean Wahl, A Human Existence and Transcendence(s)

The philosophy of existence is a philosophy of transcendence.

On the evening of Saturday, December 4, 1937, Jean Wahl (1888–1974), professor of philosophy at the Sorbonne, spoke to the Société française de philosophie. His topic: "Subjectivité et transcendance."[1] The transcript of the meeting published in the society's *Bulletin* shows how historically remarkable this event was: it brought together a virtual "who's who" of the Parisian intellectual scene and beyond. Following Wahl's paper, major contributions to the discussion were offered by Léon Brunschvicg, Gabriel Marcel, René Berthelot, Nicolai Berdyaev (in exile from Russia), Siegfried Marck (in exile from Nazi Germany), and others. Letters of intervention were submitted on behalf of Martin Heidegger, Emmanuel Levinas, Karl Jaspers, Karl Löwith, Rachel Bespaloff, Denis de Rougemont, Raymond Aron, and Georges Bastide, and others, with responses from Wahl. This was an event that Emmanuel Levinas would immortalize simply as "Wahl's famous lecture."[2] Looking back from the vantage afforded by seventy-five years, one is tempted not only to affirm Levinas's judgment but to add to it by saying that this lecture was, in fact, a watershed. It galvanized and refigured perhaps the key debate of the Parisian intellectual scene of his era, namely the destiny of the notion of transcendence within the ever-broadening and self-purifying conception of immanence developing in the wake of phenomenology, especially that of Heidegger. In the lecture, Wahl expressed this key locus of reflection in the form of a question: Can there be a secular concept of transcendence that allows the thinking of the concrete existence of human being without an extrinsic appeal to an abstract divine, that is, without theology and without even the "secularization" of theological concepts? Or would such a thinking, if it were possible, shorn of every last bit of the theological, empty of every "nostalgia," and deaf to every "echo" of the religious, leave us merely with a "general theory" of existence, dehistoricized and dehumanized, a meaningless philosophy? The paper Wahl delivered that evening constitutes the first part of the third chapter of the book that is in your hands, and it doubtlessly serves as a point of orientation for this book in its entirety. The transcript of the rigorous discussion and the letters were likewise included in this book when it originally appeared, and they remain in this edition.

―――――――――

Regardless of the answer anyone would *desire* to give (or begin to give) to Wahl's question, what matters is the pause that the question requires of us and the attention it demands. In Wahl's case it would be seriously misleading to think that he posed this question as part of some program to *écraser l'infâme*, to escape from or neutralize the hegemony of the religious and theological over the meaning of human existence. That is, he did not pose it (at least in the first, motivating, place) for the sake of answering it in any one particular way. Rather, he posed it precisely because it is a philosophical question, one that gives rise to thought, and one that implicitly was giving rise to the order of thinking that dominated his day. It was a question that—*as* a question: what does it mean to be human? Does the theological wholly determine myself as one who is capable of posing and in fact does pose this question?—fundamentally shaped Jean Wahl's own thought. And to that degree, Jean Wahl uniquely embodied—if I can risk an impossible thesis—European intellectual culture of the mid-twentieth century from (and through) the Second World War to (and through) May 1968.

A corollary thesis: *Existence humaine et transcendance* embodies the thought of Jean Wahl in an exceptional if not irreplaceable way.

What have I asserted so far? (1) To reach the heart of Jean Wahl's thought one should read the present book. (2) To understand Jean Wahl means reaching a crucial level of understanding of European thought of the last century. I have also strongly suggested: (3) to understand the philosophical thinking of the last century through Jean Wahl opens up a path for us toward understanding ourselves, its heirs.

These assertions are not offered as theses to be proved, as I have already implied. They are, however, governing convictions that shape my understanding of Wahl, and they are meant to serve you as motivations for your own entrance into his thought and world which you have initiated by picking up the present book.

It is virtually a matter of public record that Jean Wahl was one of the earliest interpreters, and doubtlessly the most important, of Kierkegaard in France.[3] He was also an original thinker of no small magnitude whose influence on contemporary French philosophy could hardly be overestimated. If the former is known well enough, the latter is still barely recognized. Trained under Henri Bergson, Wahl wrote a *thèse complémentaire* on the notion of the temporal instant in Descartes.[4] His *thèse principale* was an exhaustive study of Anglo-American philosophies of pluralism, particularly the pragmatism of William James.[5] He likewise developed an important interpretation of Hegel, reading his later, famous works in continuity with his early religious writings and especially from the vantage of Kierkegaard's criticisms that highlighted the role of the anxiety of the subject in Unhappy Consciousness for Hegel's "system" as a whole.[6]

In this latter book the reader can begin to see how much Wahl's own thinking develops out of an encounter with Kierkegaard. In this encounter that came to define his philosophical legacy, Wahl brought specific concerns that he articulated under the name of *la philosophie de l'existence*, or *la philosophie existentielle*: man is a problem to himself, a problem that cannot be answered except by posing the problem as an insoluble one. He poses this problem by posing the question of being, and he poses the question of being only by posing the question of himself. The perceptive reader could perhaps already intuit that it was not Kierkegaard alone, however. One could almost say that (if he is not directly on the page) Kierkegaard was behind every page that Wahl wrote, and further, Heidegger and Hegel stand there with him. Whatever Wahl's disagreements with these philosophers (and with Hegel in particular disagreement runs deep), each one of these thinkers lived his philosophy; their thought was an example of a deep and singular articulation of "metaphysical experience."

There is of course a set of standard views of Wahl's work: first, there is the one that considers Wahl primarily as an *interpreter* of Kierkegaard with no lasting philosophical contribution of his own, and, further, sees his philosophy as simply an attempt to secularize Kierkegaard or appropriate him to a general existentialism. Second, there is the complementary view that sees Wahl's significance primarily in his central, auxiliary role as an educator (in whose debt lies a generation at least of French philosophers). Both of these views are profoundly true.[7] Wahl was in fact an early and influential mediator of the thought of Kierkegaard, Hegel, *and* Heidegger in French philosophy. To be fair, American philosophy—"pragmatism," in the form of its most eminent representative, William James—would need to be added to this list.[8] As the present book makes abundantly clear, Wahl ceaselessly wrestled with each one of these figures, seeking not only to understand them more and more adequately, but also—more importantly, at least in his own mind—to understand the significance of their thought, to assess and to respond to their philosophical ideas. The present book also makes plain Wahl's still important insight regarding abundant parallels between German and French philosophy and Anglo-American philosophy (in the forms of pragmatism and process philosophy especially).

As is perhaps already made patent enough, Wahl was much more than an "existentialist," and his importance should not be tied to the fate of that "movement" of twentieth-century French philosophy. One very well known index of this importance merits being stated at the outset. I am thinking of Wahl's influence on his friend, Emmanuel Levinas. The central idea of *Totality and Infinity* (1961) in fact depends on Wahl's thinking about transcendence, which is found at the heart of the present book.[9] There Levinas appropriates the first term of Wahl's distinction between "transascendence" and "transdescendence" (on which more shortly), taking it to name the "metaphysical desire" for the Other that describes the logic of disproportionate alterity and the noncollapsible "distance" that (by contrast to transdescendence) it holds in place. Making explicit reference to the second chapter below ("On the Idea of Transcendence"), Levinas says with noteworthy directness: "We have drawn much inspiration from the themes evoked in that study."[10] Similarly, it may well be—and there is some indication of this in Levinas—that the second term of Wahl's account of transcendence, *transdescendence*, is an important origin of his own account of subjectivity, determined by the interiority of the Other within, that is the theme of his second major philosophical work, *Otherwise Than Being* (1974).[11] If this is the case, then Levinas's thought, in perhaps its most basic features, might be said to be first, made possible by the thought of Jean Wahl, and second, a particularly fruitful interpretation and development of it.

―――――

Existence humaine et transcendance (published in 1944) must have been written sometime between Wahl's lecture in December 1937 and June 1942, when Wahl fled to the United States in order to preserve his life. The note attached to the front page of the book by the (Swiss) publisher, reproduced above, observes that Wahl was not able to review the proofs of the book due to *"les circonstances"*—the reader will generally comprehend what circumstances these were given the date of publication: Nazi Germany seized Paris in June 1940. This event and the subsequent story of the Second World War unfolded for Jean Wahl in the following way.[12]

Wahl, who had been made professor of philosophy at the Sorbonne in 1936, was, like all Jewish teachers in Occupied France, dismissed from his post when the Sorbonne reopened in November 1940. He was brutally interrogated by the Gestapo the following year, arrested on the charge of "impertinence" (for denying, during the interrogation, that he was a "dirty Jew"), and sent to the infamous Parisian prison La Santé. He remained at La Santé for thirty-six days and was subsequently sent to the internment camp at Drancy, outside of Paris, where he remained for sixty-four days. During this time Wahl was appointed *in absentia* to the faculty of the New School for Social Research in New York City: plans were afoot to bring him to the United States through the Refugee Scholars Fund, although there seemed to be no real hope of liberating him from his imprisonment. In the meantime dysentery ran rampant through the camp, and the French police decided to release the sickest prisoners. At the last minute, Wahl, who was not sick, was added to the list: the (French) doctor of his barrack added Wahl's name after hearing through the head nurse (whose husband was an academic) of his appointment to the New School. Wahl walked through the gates the next morning. Three weeks later he had to make a harrowing flight to Vichy France in the South with the help of an underground network. After living and teaching in Mâcon and then Lyon, Wahl decided to move to the United States when it seemed that Germany would come to occupy all of France (which happened in late 1942). After a month in Casablanca waiting for a ship with Rachel Bespaloff, he arrived in Baltimore in July 1942, almost a year to the day that he was first arrested and sent to La Santé.

In the United States,[13] Wahl participated in the faculties of three institutions, Mount Holyoke College in South Hadley, Massachusetts, Smith College, and the École libre des hautes études, the French-speaking university-in-exile, founded in 1942 and attached to the New School for Social Research. Wahl taught philosophy at both Mount Holyoke and the École libre, and he lectured on French literature at Smith. His main position was at Mount Holyoke, where he lived. He helped found and lead the famous Décades de Mount Holyoke (also called Pontigny-en-Amérique), a remarkable gathering of French intellectuals in exile (such as Jacques Maritain, Gustave Cohen, and Rachel Bespaloff) and American thinkers (including, famously, poets Wallace Stevens and Marianne Moore). These meetings were modeled on the famous gatherings founded by the intellectual Paul Desjardins, the Décades de Pontigny, an annual meeting of European intellectuals at a famed Cistercian abbey in Burgundy purchased by Desjardins that ran from 1910 to 1914 and 1922 to 1939 (brought to an end by the German invasion of Poland). Wahl, whose father was a professor of English at Marseille (and in fact succeeded Mallarmé at the post), was completely at home in the English language, as is demonstrated by his many letters, English-language publications (poetry and prose), translations (including scholarly editions of English authors John Cowper Powys and Thomas Traherne and American poet Wallace Stevens), and his 1920 doctoral thesis (*thèse principale*), translated into English five years later as *The Pluralist Philosophies of England and America*.

Wahl returned to France in 1945, resumed his post at the Sorbonne, married one of his students (with whom he had three daughters, and a son who died at one month's age), and quickly returned to the center of Parisian intellectual life (e.g., he founded the Collège philosophique, served as the president of the Société française de philosophie, and directed the *Revue de m*étaphysique et de *morale*) until his death in 1974 at the age of eighty-six.[14]

Before proceeding to further remarks about Jean Wahl, his "famous lecture," and this book, it is worth reminding ourselves about the state of what I have called his "orienting question" today. It hardly needs arguing that the notion of the "secularization" of concepts is a theory that itself has an important place in the history of modern thought: an invocation of the names of Karl Löwith, Carl Schmitt, and Hans Blumenberg is sufficient to show it. Ideas within—even fundamental to and defining of—intellectual domains outside of theology (philosophy, politics, sociology, etc.) have a religious and theological origin. The fact that such a thesis does not demand immediate consent with the force of a historical fact for contemporary Western self-understanding testifies precisely to its profundity and significance—if also to our most important blind spot. Yet its importance and centrality is misunderstood if it is not properly contextualized. We ought first to say that such a place afforded to the theological—as the nourishing womb that gave (gives?) birth to reason—is a *defining feature* of Western intellectual culture.[15] More acutely and more adequately put: Western philosophy from the beginning to the present day is itself only intelligible as a "genealogy of the theological." The implications of such a thesis are debatable; its historicity, it seems to me, is not. The embrace and negation of the theological/religious dimension in Western intellectual culture are only two integral points of dialectic within the domain named by this genealogy. Jean Wahl expresses precisely this in his *Traité de métaphysique*: "Through their proximity to this idea [of God] all these problems [evil, the will, freedom, personality, one and the many, the good] have often taken on a profundity that they would not have been able to have otherwise, for human thought has come to maturity within what could be called a theological context, sometimes on account of this context, sometimes against it."[16]

English theologian John Milbank has recently expressed the logic and implications of his version of a thesis corollary to this broader one: "An entity called 'philosophy' has never . . . really existed in pure independence from religion or theology. . . . [T]he idea, or rather, the illusion, of a sheerly autonomous philosophy is twice over the historical invention of certain modes of theology itself."[17] The features of this *particular* thesis (as "genealogy of modernity") are not our concern here, but rather the recognition by the thesis of the wholly modern character of a rigid division of philosophy and theology, and even the (typically unrecognized) theological origin of such a division. Regardless of that, Jean Wahl is probably rightly understood to lie somewhere within the continuum of this defining Western dialectic. I should like to say—and I think the present book is a case in point—that he would be most deeply understood, however, to embody the entire dialectic in his philosophy. Extrapolating from this assertion as a general point of orientation, let us recall a few fundamental facts.

Reference to Thales's "first word" of philosophy is a commonplace: "All things are full of gods."[18] Aristotle represented the classical view of the philosopher's critical continuity with mythic-ritual consciousness in his famous sentence in the opening paragraphs of the *Metaphysics*, "Even the lover of myth is in a sense the lover of wisdom, for myth is composed of wonders."[19] The critical nature of philosophical response to myth was itself religious, a matter of concern for the adequate representation of the divine by human thought.[20] Hence for the ancients philosophy was a mode of religious life, and in fact—and here lies the philosophical revolution in its most potent center in Plato—philosophy was conceived as accomplishing precisely that which the cults of the gods could only tragically emphasize as impossible: knowledge of the ultimately real and human salvation.[21] Philosophy is itself a "religious" enterprise; not simply a "spiritual exercise,"[22] but a religious one, meant to accomplish that which the religions sought. There is more.

The "religiosity" of philosophy, its peculiar piety, involves what I would call the apophatic "transfer of intelligibility" between thought thinking its object and thought thinking about itself (precisely *as* thinking about its object), an endless, restless dialectic of reason, most profoundly endless and most acutely restless when it turns to its most challenging and most basic task (thinking God).[23] It is well known that philosophy is born out of and continues as a "critique" of the idols generated by mythic religious experience, from antiquity to the modern period (Kant, Nietzsche, Hegel, Heidegger, Derrida, Nancy, Marion . . . all the same from this vantage). What is not well understood is the evidently permanent dialectic joining *logos* and *mythos*: the more primary narrative order of human culture provides the initial orientating framework of intelligibility that makes possible the birth *and* sustenance of conceptual rationality. The basic narratives communities (and individuals, in fact) tell provide a "pretheoretical" understanding of the total human order offering "extratheoretical" access to our fundamental transhistorical coordinates of origin and end.[24] At the classical origin of the Western tradition (and there are analogies with others),[25] philosophy is conceived as an intellectual penetration into the divinity, into that *logos* that gives first and final meaning to all that is, and it is just as fundamentally conceived as a life lived in accord with this *logos*.[26] When reason comes to ask what it itself is, this accomplishment of the ambition of the religious in the *bios theoretikos* gives an account of reason as such that receives its own intelligibility from the divine realm itself, conceived, minimally, as its origin, constant milieu, and end. Reason is all the more rational as it is all the more divine. A crucial implication of this is that any account of reason is ultimately only as good as its conception of God (and vice versa).

This vantage explains why the early Christian thinkers from the second to fifth centuries understood Christianity as the "true philosophy": the Incarnation discloses the effulgent mystery of the God known only in a shadowy way through the world of experience reflected on by the philosophers.[27] In its early theoretical reflection on itself, Christianity understood itself as accomplishing the philosophical "enlightenment" anticipated by the greatest philosophers.[28]

From here it is not hard to advance the thesis that this apophatic "transfer of intelligibility" from religious experience to rationality as such is basic to philosophical traditions from antiquity to the present. I mention two representative examples, one ancient and one contemporary. If the so-called *Chaldean Oracles* were, for the late Platonists from Porphyry to Damascius (and in this they were only repeating Aristotle in a new key), considered to hold the intelligible content of philosophy under mythic form,[29] then contemporary philosophy in France has come to realize something similar in its own unique intellectual context: for these thinkers, religious phenomena provide, by their very nature, an absolute qualification of rationality, even to the point of offering the data of revelation as paradigmatic for phenomenological intelligibility as such.[30] One influential instantiation of this sensibility is the strange attunement of Jacques Derrida's "deconstruction" with the "negative theology" at the heart of traditional religious reflection developed by Jean-Luc Nancy's ongoing *Deconstruction of Christianity* (2005–).[31] Here Nancy holds the wholly classical supposition that revelation, or at least religious rationality, contains within itself the conditions for transfiguring philosophical speculation. But he emphasizes that this comes with a cost: in the passage of transfer demanded and goaded by religion's intelligible character it sows the seeds of its own undoing since the capturing of revelation in concepts is always only historically conditioned interpretation and therefore irreducibly tainted by all too human categories. With this, Nancy lies in direct continuity with Heidegger and in fact only acutely expresses the latter's most fundamental presuppositions: if "God" only contaminates the thought of being (the task of human thinking for Heidegger) and vice versa,[32] then any adequately human thought of God can only be negative. God is the abyss into which every idea cast by the human mind disappears. Because every possible thought of God falls short, the most faithful human thought to God is the thought that refuses every thought of God. "To philosophize!" declares Heidegger, "and in so doing to be genuinely religious."[33] Yet, as philosophy this genuinely religious character is *not* a matter of "religious ideology and fantasy." Heidegger continues: "Philosophy in its radical, self-posing questionability, must be *a-theistic* as a matter of principle. Precisely on account of its basic intention, philosophy must not presume to possess or determine God. The more radical philosophy is, the more determinately is it on a path away from God; yet precisely in the radical actualization of the 'away,' it has its own difficult proximity to God."[34] Nancy's "deconstruction" only pushes this (Heideggerian) "difficult proximity" forward. As he says in the opening lines of *Dis-Enclosure*: "It is . . . a question of opening mere reason up to the limitlessness that constitutes its truth."[35]

To the side of Nancy's project is the current phenomenological milieu in France, still fundamentally shaped by its fruitful beginning in the so-called theological turn effected in the latter half of the twentieth century by Husserl's major French interpreters. For these thinkers, it is the transcendence of the divine appearing to a human rationality always seeking to catch up with it that precisely serves as the first and final condition for an adequate conception of human rationality itself. The "postphenomenological" viewpoint of Nancy is one with that of the theological turn inasmuch as both are self-conscious heirs of Heidegger.[36]

The latter "phenomenological" position, however (at least under the pen of Jean-Luc Marion), considers Heidegger as a representative of the problem to be overcome, instantiating a major moment of the a priori conscription of the possible (the essence of "metaphysics"), which is based on the individual philosopher's predilections and *not* what may and/or in fact does itself appear.[37] In a way analogous to Schelling's critique of Hegel, Nancy likewise falls under this critique of the metaphysical inasmuch as he fails to see his "deconstruction" as a negative *praeparatio evangelica*, as a gateway to truly religious faith that explicates the intelligibility of the phenomenon par excellence, divine "revelation."[38]

This conversation between Nancy and Marion (which extends an earlier one between Derrida and Marion on the concept of the gift) concerns ultimately the equivalence of the truly religious and the truly philosophical.[39] It reached a critical moment in a debate held at the Institut Catholique de Paris in 2011.[40] This debate showed that what is finally at stake for phenomenologist Jean-Luc Marion and "postphenomenologist" Jean-Luc Nancy alike is the *unity of human rationality itself* and a fundamental renewing of the Western philosophical project. In this case, it is precisely the evidential force of revelation that "saves" the unity of reason. The upshot seems to be that, at this point of origin, where revelation provides its own intelligibility and creates the conditions for human reason, these two distinct discourses, theology and philosophy, are fully identified; and that, paradoxically, this formal unity is the condition for their material distinction. This conception of the relation of reason and revelation in the primary transfer of intelligibility from revelation to reason must be conceived, paradoxically, as itself based on an original transfer from reason to revelation in which reason recognizes itself in (an always more original transfer from) revelation and discerns its inscrutable origin and endless completion.[41]

Stepping back from phenomenology to European philosophy more generally, countercurrents in twentieth-century political theory had already acknowledged this direction of the transfer of intelligibility as well: Carl Schmitt argued in his famous *Politische Theologie* (1922) that "all significant concepts of modern theory of the state are secularized theological concepts,"[42] while Ernst Kantorowicz in *The King's Two Bodies* (1957) extended Henri de Lubac's *"corpus mysticum"* thesis (*Corpus Mysticum*, 1949) to show that the theological structure of the sacred body, originally demarcating the matrix of the sacramental presence of Christ in the church and Eucharist, is progressively transferred to the political domain as a metaphor to underwrite political structures at the foundation of modernity.[43] German philosopher Hans Blumenberg, in his massive project of "metaphorology," observed that the philosophical *questions* that modern philosophy has sought to answer by conscripting the "paradigms" inherited from medieval theological reflection are themselves perennial and necessary. He argued as a consequence for the "legitimacy" of the transfer of intelligibility from sacred to secular domains at the root of modernity.[44] These acknowledgments of the paradigmatic influence of the theological and the religious on theoretical reflection outside of their realm is presently the new orthodoxy of critical theory, as summarized and advanced in the work of the literary theorist and philosopher William Franke, whose own position is not far from Nancy's.[45]

Look at how far we have come. The old orthodoxy of modern liberal theology conceived of the relation of revelation and reason, or their respective discourses, theology and philosophy, as a one-way street. Certainly since Harnack's *History of Dogma* (1885–98), the historians thought that heavy traffic runs from the philosophical to theological realms. For Harnack, early Christianity was infected by an alien influence of Greek philosophy on the Jewish teaching of Jesus and the apostles. The task of the historian in his view was to separate the "pure" Gospel from this alien influence. Harnack's view was grounded in what today has come to be seen as a questionable presupposition regarding the "essence" of Christianity (rooted in the aberrations of nineteenth-century German Protestantism rather than in what the historical texts contain to be thought), and yet Harnack was right to see the all-pervasive influence of Greco-Roman categories on Christian thought. Under the aegis of Origen's concept of the "spoils of Egypt," theologians have by right borrowed concepts from outside of the biblical domain in order to aid them in the expression of Christian doctrine (whether the "Neoplatonism" of the church fathers, the Aristotelianism of the late medievals, or the post-Kantian "Idealism" of Balthasar or Barth). Yet at least since H. Austryn Wolfson's groundbreaking historical study, *Philosophy of the Church Fathers* (1956), it has become apparent that the influence is profoundly reciprocal.[46] According to Wolfson, the challenge of new Christian convictions about God, the world, and man refigured reason from within. More recently, David Bentley Hart, in his *Atheist Delusions* (2009), has argued with force that the pressure chamber of dogmatic debate in the classical era of Christian doctrine transfigured the most basic concepts of Western philosophy (substance, person, relation, etc.).[47] This fundamental revision is now, arguably, the majority view among historians.[48]

What matters here is that, in either case, the transfer of intelligibility between the theological and philosophical has been seen to be a defining feature of the Western tradition.

Returning, finally, to contemporary phenomenology centered in France: this tradition in some of its main figures has likewise come to realize something strikingly similar in its own unique intellectual context: religious phenomena, in providing the greatest challenge to reason by virtue of their vertigo-inducing transcendence, also expand rationality itself by virtue of their inexhaustible intelligibility.[49] This dynamism of the deconstruction and reconstruction of rationality by religious phenomenality (and subsequently theological rationality), has led these thinkers to reflect on the relation between philosophy and theology, which are understood no longer as two distinct and self-sufficient domains, but rather as always already deeply implicated and intertwined. What is finally at stake, therefore, with Jean-François Courtine's conception of *effets en retour* (countereffects),[50] Jean-Yves Lacoste's *frontière absente* (missing boundary),[51] Emmanuel Falque's *choc en retour* (counterblow),[52] Jean-Luc Marion's conception of *certitudes négatives* (negative certainties),[53] is the unity of *human* rationality across the domains of philosophy and theology. As Jean-Luc Marion has argued, it is precisely the evidential force of revelation that saves the unity of reason and offers coherence to the philosophical response to the mystery of existence.[54] After the "end of metaphysics" (the failure of classical abstract principles to command philosophical and religious attention) that has culminated in the "death of God" (the normatively uncompelling nature of traditional religious belief), contemporary French phenomenologists are inscribed in a program that refigures the traditional "*logos* doctrine" of Christian faith opened particularly by the letters of Saint Paul and the Gospel of John: that the *logos tou theou* (Word of God) incarnate in Jesus of Nazareth is the very *logos*, or principle of intelligibility, studied and sought, if only fragmentarily, by the philosophers.

On the face of it, Jean Wahl stands closer to Nancy, Franke, or Heidegger than to Marion, Milbank, or Kierkegaard. Yet regardless of how we would wish to answer that question (which depends on our personal metaphysical allegiances, as it were), all the evidence suggests that in Wahl's case the answer is not so straightforward. Wahl's impassioned discussion with Gabriel Marcel after his paper "Subjectivity and Transcendence" is worth referring to inasmuch as it can give us a point of reference out of the present volume.[55] Marcel, in taking issue with Wahl on the possibility of an a-theological, nonreligious concept of transcendence, suggests that the true "peril" involved in linking philosophy of existence too directly with theology is *not* for the reason that the theological tends to inform and hence pollute the "philosophical" description of human existence. Precisely because, he says, theological ideas "did not fall from heaven" but are generated out of human experience, they are, in fact, always of major philosophical significance. Rather, the true peril results when the philosopher is tied (whether implicitly or explicitly, negatively or positively) to an "overly determined theology." *This* is where the "act of betrayal" of the philosophical enterprise precisely lies, according to Marcel. In other words, when the philosopher thinks he knows what theology says, and develops his philosophy as a response to *that* theology, he runs the risk of building a counterfeit philosophy on top of a vapid theology, a theology that he already rejects but to which his philosophy remains invisibly bound. The problem, Marcel continues, occurs therefore when the philosopher stands on "ideological terrain," *not only* accepting a predetermined, reductive conception of theology without sufficient interrogation into it, for which (Marcel seems to suggest here) the theological is a mere "idea," problematically insufficient, not worthy of what believers conceive when they think of and worship God; *but also* desiring to throw *that* flat picture to the wind for the sake of another picture that only gratifies one's own short-sighted agenda.[56] Hence he says rhetorically in response to Wahl's proposal of a critical distance from theology for the sake of a possible secular transcendence: "It seems to me that you are using the words 'God' and 'theology' in a determined hyper-Christian sense. . . . [But] I do not think that the idea of transcendence stretched to the limit is secularizable." Perhaps, therefore, a philosophy intrinsic to the religious enterprise could be imagined as more philosophical for that reason; only an (onto-theological) account of "God" set in opposition to the world, as if a mere being within it (a conceptual idolatry in the religious sense; an "overly determined" theology), would require a philosophy at odds with and in "competition" with the theological for the meaning of human being. For Marcel this means at the very least that any possible account of transcendence (which, however multiplied, still always points to an ever-greater unity beyond) is always "religious" inasmuch as our concept of transcendence names the unnameable, the divine mystery that is always a possibility.

On my reading, Marcel and Wahl are not as far removed from one another as would seem first to be the case.[57]

Raising the question of the possibility of an alterity that is without religious appeal, "not necessarily the God of the religions nor even of their heterodoxies," as Wahl desires to do, is nevertheless wholly distinct from actually carving out a space for a purely "secular" transcendence. Wahl desired to propose a new or renewed groundless ground of transcendence in the "immediacy of feeling" which would redefine the ecstatic structure of human existence in its passage out of itself into the ever-receding Unknown where the differentiation of transascendence and transdescendence is finally erased. This account, which he *did* intend to precede the religious expression of human existence, is not, however, "secular," not an attempt to speak the human in its essential finitude apart from the contrast with divine transcendence, as it is in Heidegger.[58] On the contrary, as Emmanuel Levinas points out, for Wahl "transcendence [is] prior to being": the ecstatic character of human existence that makes humans the site of "metaphysical experience" is only flattened and made abstract by the "isolating" distinction between "Being" and "subjectivity."[59] "Consciousness and thought spring up, then, in an event they neither exhaust nor encompass, and which brings them about . . ."[60] As we will see, Wahl calls this intersection of transcendence and subjectivity the "metaphysical reality" in which we "bathe": it is as much "religious" as "secular," and in fact to understand the human being we must do away with that distinction in order that we may discern the fact that we are marked by a sudden and permanent alterity that defines us but ever eludes us. Wahl was not averse to the question of God, but he was always concerned to keep it a question, and even a most pressing one.

Elsewhere in his writings Wahl makes it much clearer that he does not avow a simplistic opposition between finite "names" (of religions, philosophies) and the Unknown mystery in which we are immersed ("names" to be shed like husks once the mystical union is achieved), but rather always feels compelled to keep the names and absolute alterity in perpetual play. On the one hand, he says in a (significantly undated) letter:

> Yes, I am a bearer of a Jewish tradition—as much as the Hellenic; and Judaism, both by itself and through the New Testament—which is Jewish and Hellenic—influences all Western thought.
>
> A community of suffering unites me to other Jews. . . .
>
> I am a non-unified [*non-unifié*] Jew; I do not care to be standardized [*unifié*], except under certain aspects—perhaps the highest ones . . .[61]

This "suffering" is inseparably, and infinitely problematically, both the suffering of the Jews at the hands of others (reaching its unthinkable nadir in Wahl's own lifetime), and the "suffering" of election, of "bearing" the Name of God. These "highest" aspects that unify Wahl with his Jewish tradition are lived by him in a non-"standardized" way, precisely through the practice of philosophy, in the double-tradition that defines the Western inheritance. Hence, in response to the question "Do you believe in God?" in a late interview on Swiss radio, Wahl answers: "I have to hesitate before responding. I believe that this question cannot be answered without following what I call . . . the philosopher's way. I can only answer this question by affirming God, negating him, reaffirming him, and finally by re-negating and always being unable to decide [*et en s'interrogeant toujours*]."[62] Wahl here alludes to the threefold "way" of classical "negative theology" that critiques or "negates" the original affirmations of faith out of a fidelity to the transcendence of what is originally given (the data of revelation), thereby returning through critique to a hyperaffirmation beyond negation, a critical appropriation of the original data of faith.[63] But he adds a fourth moment, a hyperphilosophical return to the negation by passing *through* the excess of hyperaffirmation of the classical position. Being *en s'interrogeant toujours*—"always wondering," "always questioning oneself," "always unable to decide"—is the path of the philosopher.

On the other hand, his 1945 poem "Invocation" attests to a lived faith, albeit simultaneously removed from and problematically joined to the faith of the community of believers:

> O Jésus, non pas toi
> Qu'ils invoquent, mais toi que je ressens ce soir,
> Toi brûlure, présent infini, juge et frère.
> Travaille en moi et doucement manie mon âme.[64]

> O Jesus, not you
> Whom they invoke, but you whom I feel tonight,
> You burning, immeasurably here, judge and brother.
> Work in me and sweetly touch my soul.

Wahl's resolute determination to inhabit an impossible religious space of indecision between Catholicism and Judaism is an attempt to be faithful to himself and, paradoxically, to God.[65] In a poem entitled "Atheism," only recently published, Wahl expresses his position thus:

> L'athée est bien plus étroitement uni à Dieu
> Par son refus où Dieu s'affirme lui-même
> Que le croyant par sa croyance.[66]

> The atheist is even more directly united to God
> By his refusal in which God affirms himself
> Than the believer through his belief.

Similarly he says in a late interview published in the same article: "I am not absolutely sure that I do not believe at all, since I [already] said that we bathe in a metaphysical reality. Consequently I am not . . . a complete non-believer, as some would think after some things that I have said. There is a tension within me between unbelief and belief."[67] This enactment of his own "difficult proximity" to God (so far removed from what may only be called, in its light, the pseudodifficult "proximity" of Heidegger's easy atheism) Wahl *lives philosophically* by raising questions, by "wondering" or "always asking/interrogating himself" (*s'interrogeant toujours*), and by reaching (as it were) the essential existential situation of humanity where the limits of concepts and theses are revealed at the same time as their permanence and necessity. A resolute remaining in the space of indecision is, for Wahl, the only adequate decision *for* the Ineffable in which he finds himself always already "bathed."

On my reading Wahl desires simply to express the human "situation" in its radical limitations that press into us at every point but which we always seek to overcome—precisely by undoing the "names" we afford to the Unknown. Wahl, in other words, only ever wanted to give the question its proper due. If that was not philosophy's task, it was his particular philosophical task. In the case of transcendence, we do not know that we know even if we do actually know . . . Human beings are not divine; we cannot determine the possible by fiat. This impossibility of closing down the possible is a basic feature of ourselves, the paradoxical intersection of "subjectivity and transcendence."

———————

The conjunction of these last two words may be the key to Wahl's thought. For him, they are a crucial conceptual component of any philosophy adequate to the human situation. A few remarks are therefore in order about his famous paper, "Subjectivity and Transcendence," mentioned above. These remarks will also serve as a first point of orientation to the book.

Wahl begins this paper by explaining that for Kierkegaard, "subjectivity," or rather, the "tension" that creates subjectivity, is created by the presence of "transcendence." According to Wahl, the way of thinking that marks the Danish philosopher (as much as Heidegger and Jaspers as well) is explicated precisely in the new conjunction of these two ideas. The traditional conception of the subject as "soul," that is, as locus of the presence of a divine transcendence, is completely rethought by Kierkegaard: here we do not have an "expansion" or "overflow" of excess in the relation of subjects human and divine, but rather an encounter, a "force of negation," an "opposition of individualities" that are "irreducible" one to the other. This awareness of subjectivity (and its problematic) is a *defining feature* of modern thought, and makes Kierkegaard an irreplaceable figure in Wahl's understanding. Kierkegaardian "anxiety" is completely distinct from any traditional approach to transcendence—marked, classically in Plotinus, by the *confluence* of the soul and the divine—in that for him the soul is not only self-enclosed as an absolute *individuality*, but further, is self-enclosed as an individuality *with freedom*. In the *Études kierkegaardiennes*, Wahl observes that the disrupting presence of God's absolute transcendence is the most constitutive element of human subjectivity, the whole tension of which is marked by the problem of how to convert this Other, who menaces and challenges one's subjectivity to its foundations, into the very condition for one's own beatitude.[68] Here the traditional metaphysical problematic of the relation of the infinite and the finite, in their absolute distinction yet necessary relation, is radicalized by Kierkegaard through the insertion of the human will, in all its infinity, into the heart of the problematic. This insertion gives rise to what Wahl calls the "presence of evil," the fundamental ambiguity of this presence of the Infinite which raises anxiety to the second power, doubling the tension intrinsic to anxiety inherent in the Kierkegaardian account of subjectivity. This ambiguity or uncertainty raises the possibility that Wahl identifies of *kinds* of transcendence: transcendence is not (necessarily) singular, is not exhaustively identified with the divinity alone. For Kierkegaard at least these modalities of transcendence still remain traditional, being either relation with the divine or with the diabolical (though each—and this is what makes Kierkegaard "modern"—is defined by the *movement* of the human will in accomplishing itself as good or evil). Here emerges Wahl's famous distinction between "transascendence" and "transdescendence." In its light he makes manifest the entire problematic of the modern concept of transcendence: namely, that *the erasure of the term or goal or goad of the movement of transcendence calls into question the very tension within the act that defines it.*[69]

We reach the heart of Wahl's remarks in his presentation of what he calls Kierkegaard's "description" of the "phenomenon of belief" (167) which immediately follows. As Wahl puts it, it is the presence of an unassimilable transcendence that constitutes subjectivity, and further, an absolute other impossibly rendered temporal, or in other words, to risk Heideggerian language, *an* ontological reality, *the* ontological reality, become an ontic participant in history, and in the midst of this contingency constituting the ontological structure of human subjectivity as belief. The very conditions of finite experience are crossed, contradicted, and reordered by a (the?) religious *event*. This relation, marked by the "absolute protest against immanence" (to use the relevant phrase of Kierkegaard's) is the locus of subjectivity's break with rationality (as defined by the ontological distinction) inasmuch as in our desire for beatitude or salvation we sense or feel that our relation with the historical (more precisely: the eternal made historical) becomes the condition for our salvation. Here, in the famously termed "crucifixion of reason," we take leave of rational control of our existence and destiny. This absolute other in its eternity is indefinable and unreachable; it comes into existence, becomes real, through our "subjective" relation with it in history. Now this relation with something external, the absolute in history, is paradoxically revealed in and through the absolutely immanent relation within the individual and defines subjectivity itself: it is only our "absolute passion," the depth of our subjective interiority, that *manifests* the reality of this relation with the most objective of all realities, the Absolute, and further, it is the quality of this passion as absolute—that is, the new depth of our subjectivity—that alone "proves" or gives pressing evidence for the truth or objectivity of belief (namely, that we are in a real relation with the Absolute itself). The paradox of such subjective "objectivity" (or objective "subjectivity") is an explication of the nature of this paradoxical Presence. As Wahl says, "The intensity of this relation is such that, in the same way that we enter into it, it gives to us this other term, which in a sense can never be given" (167). In this way there is an intensification of mutual reciprocity between subjectivity and objectivity, between immanence and transcendence: the deeper, the more absolute subjectivity becomes, the more the objectivity of the relation is manifest. Only the greatest subjectivity, belief, can reveal the Objectivity par excellence, the Absolute.

The "phenomenon of belief" is therefore marked by exit toward the other and passionate interiority at once. In the last pages of *Traité de métaphysique* (1953), Wahl summarizes his sprawling text by an analysis of the concept of transcendence in the history of philosophy that develops what he already adumbrates here in 1937. There Wahl risks a simple categorization and observes that the tradition of philosophy has discerned three types of transcendence, corresponding to three phases of its history: (1) ancient, (2) modern, and (3) contemporary (let us say "postmodern" or "hypermodern" *avant la lettre*).

First, there is transcendence conceived as the *Absolute*, the separated *logos* of Heraclitus, the Good beyond being of Plato, the One of Plotinus, the nameless one beyond the one of Damascius, and so forth. Second, there is transcendence as *transcendental*, evacuated of content, rooted in Kant's separation of transcendence into two kinds: first, the transcendent prohibited to human access; and then, transcendence appropriate to our finite state, understood as conditions for the intelligibility of immanence, otherwise said, that which must be in order to make sense of our experience. Third, for Wahl writing in 1953, there is the intensification of this transcendental turn in "intentional" transcendence, understood as the structural elaboration of immanence itself, as movement toward alterity, as found in Husserl's elaboration of consciousness correlated to the world and objects in the world, and then expanded to being and beings in the world by Heidegger.

Wahl discerns two dangers revealed by this little history of transcendence, one that negates immanence or concrete existence for the sake of the transcendent—a danger of classical accounts—and one that, on the other hand, negates the term or intentional object of transcendence—a danger of modern/contemporary accounts. The upshot of his discussion there, under primarily Kierkegaardian inspiration (as we have seen), argues that any adequate account of transcendence, understood as a permanent dimension of *human* existence, must recognize a constitutive tension that cannot be reduced but at the expense of transcendence itself. The concept, he says, contains an essential "ambiguity," for it must mean at once the "ever unattainable *terme* of our thought and effort of thought" and also "this very effort itself towards the *terme*" (645). That is to say, transcendence is indelibly marked by a fundamental duality that is permanent and irresolvable: the duality of, on the one hand, transcendence as transcending, as the ecstatic structure of temporal movement, that is, as finitude; and, on the other hand, transcendence as *terme* (term, terminus, limit, or end), the ungraspable reality beyond the movement that inspires it, without which the movement collapses into itself and is no longer transcend-*ing*. Heidegger, after Husserl and more fundamentally after Kant, reduced transcendence to the singular aspect of transcending, full stop: human existence, on this account, is an act of opening, a sheer ecstatic structure of "movement toward" the possible. The all-determining master concept of the "ontological difference," if I could add an elaboration to Wahl's thoughts here, makes transcendence as *terme* a priori impossible; on this account, transcendence is and can only ever be an aspect of immanence conceived as a groundless finitude without a contrast to the infinite or eternal that could underwrite its own meaningfulness. Does this, however, not close down the questioning before it could open itself sufficiently—ruling the question of God or at least its relevance out of play in advance, and making God's meaningful appearing such as attested to or affirmed in religion a priori *impossible*, thereby legislating that the distinction it recognizes and spreads univocally over the totality of the given is most fundamental and the only one possible?

Yet the fundamental problem "posed by the idea of transcendence itself," says Wahl, is "to know whether we can maintain both senses of the term"—which means explicitly in the context of post-Heideggerian thought, "to know if the movement of transcendence implies the idea of a terminus [*terme*] that is irreducible to us and which transcends us" (646). The question is rephrased by Wahl as an alternative between two options, almost classically articulated: "Is that which is conceived or felt by us as transcendent independent of our minds or is it a property of the human mind itself, projecting beyond itself what we could call its highest point?" (646). Post-Heideggerian thought is marked by the second alternative, in Wahl's terms, of "transcending transcendence and returning to immanence" (646).[70] On Wahl's account, making this decision determinative of our philosophy fails to heed the most important aspect of philosophical inquiry, the *permanent insolubility* of its most basic problems: "If one chooses too explicitly," he says, "he risks destroying the value [of transcendence] and that which composes the very root of the problem" (646). In other words, to put it in Kantian language and perhaps too harshly, this is the point where one passes over from philosopher to dogmatician. By contrast to Heidegger, Wahl sought to "retain transcendence" in the return to immanence.

With this critique, Jean Wahl, at least I would argue, anticipates an important dimension of contemporary Continental thought, which has recently been quite daringly called by an Anglo-Saxon observer, "transgressive realism": that our contact with reality at its most real dissolves our preconceived categories and gives itself on its own terms, that truth as *novelty* is not only possible, though understood as such only ex post facto, but is in fact the most valuable and even paradigmatic kind of truth, defining our human experience.[71] The fundamental realities determinative of human experience and hence philosophical questioning—the face of the other, the idol, the icon, the flesh, the event, to use Jean-Luc Marion's well-known conceptual apparatus, and also divine revelation, freedom, life, love, evil, and so forth—exceed the horizon of transcending-immanence and give more than what it, on its own terms, allows, thereby exposing that its own conditions are not found in itself and opening from there onto more essential terrain. The question raised here concerns precisely the *terme* of the movement of transcending, that which gives it to itself in its movement: can there be two distinct manners of understanding this idea? One, the Heideggerian mode, proposes that the *terme* cannot be given, can only at best be perpetually delayed (as in Derrida), and its nonappearing, its absence and impossibility the means of the absolute expansion of the movement of immanence itself; the other, a Kierkegaardian mode, says that the *terme* is given, but given as nongiven, and yet nongiven because excessively given, that is, given *paradoxically*, given as perpetually escaping the grasp of the movement of transcending within immanence, founding it, and given thereby all the more radically.

Jean Wahl stands, and attempts to remain, at the fork of this path.

Transcendence, in sum, is here marked by two elements: (1) *the terme of transcendence*, the presence of the other, and the condition for the movement of immanence itself; and (2) *the movement of transcendence* interior to subjectivity or passion, which is the condition for the manifestation of the "absolute" within the conditions of historical finitude. We could almost say, as a principle: so much transcendence, so much finitude, *and vice versa.* The transcendent in itself is irresolvably joined to the transcendent in immanence, but this irresolvability requires the noncollapsibility of the difference between them, since, if it collapses, one of the essential elements of transcendence is lost. And it is this irresolvability, finally, that forms one-half of the problematic of human existence named by transcendence. The other half is articulated by the corollary distinction between transascendence and transdescendence.

This paper, "Subjectivity and Transcendence," shows that for Wahl, the phenomenon of belief proposes itself as an intensification of the concept of transcendence, and, indeed, the locus of the phenomenon of transcendence par excellence, for its terminus or object and its movement are absolute: its kind of transcendence proposes itself as a model or archetype for every phenomenon of transcendence in experience; the phenomenon of belief gives us the most transcendent of transcendences. In this way it is tempting to suggest that Wahl anticipates the basic feature of the so-called theological turn in French phenomenology since for the latter, likewise, religious phenomena give reason a paradigmatic image of itself.[72] I mentioned at the beginning the fact that Wahl rightly and profoundly understood philosophy engaged in a dialectic interior to the religious context, since, whether we like it or not, the idea of God is the most dramatically intensifying concept for philosophical reflection.[73] In the present context of Kierkegaard's singular significance, Wahl demonstrates how central Kierkegaard's thought is for this very breakthrough: "The most important aspect of the thought of Kierkegaard ... is that the religious consciousness is ... our own subjectivity, intensified to its highest point by its relation with the Absolute Other."[74] Here Wahl stands with Kierkegaard, on the other side of Heidegger, we could almost say, waiting at the fork in the road for the proponents of the "theological turn" to discover Heidegger's *metaphysical* infidelity (through an a priori restriction of the possible) to the basic task of phenomenology: "to let what shows itself be seen from itself, just as it shows itself from itself," and nothing else.[75]

According to Wahl it is the Kierkegaardian concept of *anxiety,* intrinsic to belief, which furthers this essential religio-philosophical *antinomy.* Kierkegaardian anguish is a product of the presence of the divine other whose "impossible" ontic presence, as an appearance in history in the repetition of faith, is ontologically constitutive of the believer's subjectivity itself. This much is clear. Yet the anxiety is compounded by the fact that this presence that somehow exceeds the ontico-ontological difference is a tension that is not collapsible within the historical horizon within which faith has its raison d'être. The presence of the Infinite pushes the tension that marks finitude to deeper limits. The further intensification of anxiety arrives from out of this paradoxical presence: the *terme* or object of transcendence, the condition for the movement of transcending, is through and through ambiguous. Faith is therefore only possible by virtue of *doubt*, by the *absence* of the object of faith, an absence that paradoxically registers its presence, precisely within the horizon of *faith*. Belief subsists therefore in uncertainty, inseparable from unbelief. "Belief," says Wahl, "is never sure of being in the presence of God" ("Subjectivité et transcendance," 167). It is the ambiguity of the *terme* of transcendence—not, by contrast to Heidegger, its *mere absence* or nothingness—which defines the anxiety of finitude. The anxiety about something that is greater than our distinction between something and nothing, between beings and Being, is greater than one that rests secure in the inviolability of the ontological difference, which is merely an anxiety before nothing.

Levinas's letter on the occasion of the meeting highlights what is at stake here. Here he accuses Wahl of misunderstanding the radicality of Heidegger's distinction between Being and beings, and the "overcoming" of religion that it implies: For Heidegger, "every distinction," he says, "between a [religious] beyond and a here-below is ontic and posterior to the ontological problematic," and hence, for him "the fundamental transcendence is accomplished . . . not in the passage from one being to another [even to a divine being], but rather from a being to Being itself."[76] In this so-called overcoming of onto-theology, Heidegger circumscribes the religious question as a whole. The question of Being is absolute; our relation to a specific being, even the highest Being, is secondary. Wahl's comments that follow Levinas's letter are interesting, inasmuch as they arise from an intuition that Wahl described earlier by articulating the irreducibly complex character of transcendence. Here Wahl makes the observation that Heidegger's conception of the ontological difference is purely formal, "determined," he says, "by the problem of the conditions of possibility of existence," which "does not pose its questions any more authentically or any more satisfyingly than does the criticism of reason."[77] If the problem of Being is an existential problem alone, the *humanity* of existence is drained of all its color.[78] Heidegger himself, Wahl observes, sees the *existentielle*, the ontic domain, as the necessary starting point for ontological questions (193–94). This necessary interlacing of the two domains in the phenomenon of belief demands a conception of transcendence that reflects it, which Heidegger fails to give by denying the phenomenological pertinence of the theological data manifest within the horizon of belief: in this case transcendence may or rather must be thought extrametaphysically.

In his response to Levinas, Wahl is cataloguing another false path to our conceptions of transcendence and its implications for subjectivity. There is the typical path to which Heidegger's proposal is only a response. False transcendence, on this score, is one that negates the reality of immanence and concrete existence, as in some crude Platonism for which the world of experience is only illusory, an epiphenomenon at best of the real world beyond experience. A Neoplatonic absorption of the transcending into the divine stands here as well. Here the *terme* or goal of transcendence swallows up the movement of transcendence. But the response is just as fundamental a failure. According to the other type of false transcendence, epitomized by Nietzsche or Heidegger (and we could add Derrida and Jean-Luc Nancy here), the *terme* is negated for the sake of the pure intelligibility of the transcending itself, which purports to give us a "purer" conception of finitude. For Heidegger, there can be no object or thing or person toward which our ecstatic self-transcending touches or sees or that the opening of Being discloses. The latter reduction of transcendence to the bare movement of immanence protests the former's objectification of that toward which transcendence moves. Wahl finds in Kierkegaard's phenomenology of faith a way both to recognize the ambiguity of the *terme* of transcendence as ineffable and to acknowledge the self-surpassing character of human existence, and indeed, *to intensify both sides by refusing to separate them.*[79]

It is this perspective that provokes me to suggest that Wahl antici-pates another major feature of late twentieth-century French thought: Derrida's "quasi-transcendental" concept of "*différance*" (which would arguably be a mode of transdescendence), since *différance* could prop-erly be understood as a refusal to allow transcendence as *terme* to be made absolute—it is an a priori decision, that Derrida (like Wahl) takes as the essence of human experience, to refuse to collapse transcendence as *terme* and as movement. Here, however, Wahl's anticipation already harbors implicitly the capacity to step through the hegemonic stric-ture of Derridean *différance* that refuses through infinite deferral the possibility of the gift (of the absolute *terme*), inasmuch as such a quasi transcendental only recasts the ontological difference of Heidegger in another key. Like the latter master-concept of Heidegger, this master-concept of Derrida circumscribes the field of possible experience and knowledge, not out of a fidelity to the intelligibility of what gives itself in experience, but out of a preconception of what is human, a pre-conception that itself requires justification in the light of experience. Wahl (again, after Kierkegaard) can only say that such an interroga-tion into the "humanity of man" comes most powerfully in light of the concept of God.[80] We can see this (proto) "overcoming" of decon-struction most clearly in Wahl's systematic presentation in the *Traité*. There Wahl points out in a fuller manner than he does in "Subjectiv-ity and Transcendence" the way in which Kierkegaard's paradoxical coincidence of subjectivity and objectivity (for which the deepening of subjectivity coincides with the crystallization of the object) in the phenomenology of religious belief expresses and renews the very heart of philosophical experience as it centers on God. Pointing toward the double interpretation of divine Unity in Plato's *Parmenides* (on which Wahl wrote an important commentary)[81]—the One is both beyond all and ineffable, not even "being" or "one" are finally "proper" names for it, and the One is the totality, and, again, not one, but identical with the multiple—Wahl points out that the entire task of "philosophical effort" is to unite these two hypotheses while retaining their opposition at the same time, that irreducibility of two unities, the first, of transcendence, and the second, of immanence: "to think simultaneously that the One is beyond all things and within all things."[82] Here, in other words, at the beating heart of the philosophical tradition is the highest expression of the religious attitude. Russian philosopher Sergius Bulgakov expressed this with the same fundamental force in his early masterpiece, *Unfading Light*: "That which is immanent cannot be at the same time transcendent and to that extent is not transcendent. That which is transcendent cannot be immanent to consciousness and remains beyond the limits for it. If we take these concepts in static immobility . . . the fundamental concept of religion, the idea of Divinity, is in general only a patent misunderstanding . . . burning ice, a round square, bitter honey. *But rational impossibility and contradiction are no guarantee of real impossibility*."[83] Wahl says, therefore, that "that these two conceptions of unity, one immanent and the other transcendent, are not opposed, for when we think God, we join them together, thinking at the same time that God is beyond everything, and that we live, move and have our being in him."[84]

Holding together the rationally impossible antinomy of the equal primordiality of the absolute as wholly ineffable and other *and* as eminently present to all things—more immanent to me than I am to myself, as Saint Augustine once put it—is required for an approach to the living God, the God of gods, the most divine God, the most nonidolatrous concept of God, and hence the most philosophical of philosophical ideas. Higher than possibility, separated from it, stands personality, a reality that, in its freedom, I can never comprehend. Wahl stands before this idea as a signpost at a crossroads, like Kierkegaard—for whom the true believer is always only becoming a believer, for whom doubt is intrinsic to faith—as expressed in the pseudonym Johannes Climacus, the author of the *Philosophical Fragments* and their *Concluding Unscientific Postscript*: the philosopher who stands on the threshold of faith and lives faith authentically precisely as one who knows that he cannot find himself explicitly to have or possess it.

Wahl also acknowledges the centrality of these two basic philosophical concepts to other metaphysical ideas, and he again states the deepening crystallization that occurs in the context of the concept of God: "We have already encountered these two ideas [of transcendence

and immanence] in our previous studies [that constitute the *Traité*]
pertaining to things, persons, values, and being and existence. Here,
in the notion of God, these two ideas simultaneously in conflict and
union are met once more, and at their highest point."[85]

From this vantage we can venture a response to the common critique regarding Wahl's questionable "secularization" of Kierkegaard,
an attempted detachment of the structure of Kierkegaard's ideas from
their concrete instantiation in Kierkegaard's nonphilosophy and faith,
and this, for the sake of an existentialism that prizes the concrete. Wahl
points out, as we saw, that it is of the essence of faith to doubt. The
ambivalence regarding the object of religious faith, that which makes
it faith, and not comprehending knowledge, the absence of the object,
or at least, its paradoxical kind of "ambiguous" presence that is manifest as absence, itself gives rise to the possibility, therefore, of the plurality of transcendences. Am I in the presence of an angel or demon,
God or only my desire for God, the depths of nature or a transcendent
being, and so forth?[86] The secularization, as it were, of Kierkegaard, for
Wahl only arises in this context; it is therefore not meant to rip out of
Kierkegaard's specific context the concrete character of Christian faith
for the sake of a general existentialism, suffering then from the danger that Adorno specified, namely, that abstracting Kierkegaard's existentialism from Christian theology leaves his thought open to abuse
for political ends,[87] or that danger specified by Shestov or Fondane,
namely, that separating Kierkegaard from his specific religious domain
makes him a "theorist" rather than an "existentialist" concerned with
acts of belief.[88] Rather, it is meant to intensify the problematic inherent within Kierkegaard's notion of transcendence in the first place, *to
maximize its contradictions*. For Wahl this inhabitation of the contradiction is expressive of the concrete problematic that he lived.[89] He
asked the question, a question, paradoxically as religious and authentic for his own concrete situation as Kierkegaard's Christian question,
without, *like* Kierkegaard, offering an "answer."[90] Recalling his response
to Levinas's letter in the proceedings of the meeting, Wahl first makes
what seems to be a hasty distinction between religion and existence.
He says, "For me, it is of the nature of religion to be a response. And
it is of the nature of existence first to be a question."[91] This could be

read as reifying a secularized concept of existence set over against the religious. But the difference between religion and existence does not have to be absolute—and in metaphysical experience it cannot be. Religion as a response to divine action and existence as the provocation of philosophical questioning can, and perhaps ought to be, put in relation to one another, *if* we are to escape from Heidegger's collapse of the tension of transcendence. After demonstrating the possibility of the pluralization of transcendencies, Wahl is not here reducing them back down to the singular.

The words with which he closed on the evening of December 4, 1937, reveal the heart of Wahl's conception of philosophy and the radical degree of his difference from Heidegger: "I cannot conclude by presenting a solution, because I believe that it is of the essence of existential philosophy to tell us that the problems have a value in themselves. Philosophical problems cannot be fully resolved. . . . One has to make oneself the question. And this is why I will not answer." It is the insolubility of the essential questions that philosophy's basic task is to highlight in all of their gravity, even to increase their insolubility to the point of the transformation of a life that lives from within the tension of this very insolubility. The peculiar transcendence that constitutes subjectivity, and the inherent tension within it, is the greatest philosophical question. "Existential philosophy" is nothing else for Wahl but an encounter with the impossible questions that define existence. It is therefore not the name of a movement or current or style of modern philosophy; rather, it is the nature of philosophy itself. It is this very insolubility that Heidegger himself dissolves by surrounding being with an atheist hermetical seal, thereby reducing the nature of transcendence to a movement of immanence alone. Heidegger, for Wahl, refuses to countenance philosophy's own other, its foundational manner of calling philosophy into question and thereby constituting it. It is the irresolvable tension in transcendence—that between the *terme* or end of transcendence, which always stands beyond and constitutes the self-transcending that defines radical finitude, on the one hand, and the movement of self-transcending itself, on the other—that alone does not, as Wahl says elsewhere, "destroy the value [of transcendence] and that which makes it a problem in the first place."[92] It is

Kierkegaard, for Wahl, who has already eclipsed the ontological difference and established it in the very manner of this eclipse, precisely by his new manner of thinking that, far from *resolving* the tension inherent to the problem of transcendence "in advance" (as was Heidegger's castigation), only emphasizes and elaborates it as the crucial problem.

Human Existence and Transcendence is a deceptively simple text. It is a miscellany of compositions, written in different styles, in different states of mind, and, seemingly, at different levels of completion. On the whole, one could read it as a set of notations, brought together and meant to be filled in later; from this vantage an analogy with Pascal's *Pensées* would not be misplaced. As in this latter text, the power of *Human Existence and Transcendence* is often found in what Wahl does not say as much as in what he says, in what he suggests as much as in what he asserts, and, regardless, in what he demands of the reader to think. The text, therefore, is most properly read as a set of meditations, proposals, sketches, and gestures, to be meditated on in a philosophical attitude, with a pencil in hand, by a reader willing to take his or her time, to accept Wahl's often elliptical and poetic crystallizations as (often provocative) invitations to walk with him on pathways he proposes through the perennial thickets of philosophical inquiry. To read this text, one must be prepared to think, and to think one's own thoughts after Wahl, and more often than not (as one chooses) against and beyond him.

As *Human Existence and Transcendence* shows, Wahl was a poet as much as a philosopher. A great portion of this book is given over to examining the relation between these two vocations. As much as Wahl himself was one person in whom poetry and philosophy were thought, expressed, and lived, so also one finds him given over again and again to the task of discovering the point of difference and point of unity between them. For him, the poet lives that which the philosopher always seeks to know; the poet accomplishes what the philosopher teaches. Wahl begins the book with a reference to the "poet-philosophers" Kierkegaard and Nietzsche, and he sees in them a recovery of the essence of the philosophical, a rejoining of what was only problematically separated. There is no philosophy without poetry; theory, the formation of concepts, only emerges out of *theoria*, the contemplation of reality, the experiential awareness of one's immersion in being, which is most powerfully encountered in the affective dimension of our personality. And poetry lives closer to the experience of this immersion. The logic of this encounter is described by Wahl as an "existential dialectic" (opposed to the Hegelian or Platonic kinds) that moves "from presence to dialectic, and from dialectic to ecstasy through the play of antitheses that destroy each other in order to cede their place to this ecstasy." Reasoning ("dialectic") arises out of the original affective encounter of embodied force and the feeling of resistance ("presence"). And the contradictions into which reasoning always comes to be embroiled lead it (ecstatically) to reattain the original presence in an enriched way. "It is yet," says Wahl in the later chapter "Poetry and Metaphysics," "by the union of things that contradict one another that the poet will not only be able to lead us to the beyond, but, once we have perceived this beyond, leads us back towards the here below, joining immanence to transcendence." Here we have a clear statement of Wahl's task in the present book, one, in fact, that defines his philosophical ambition. He states this concisely in two places in the preface. We can compare each one of these to two similar statements found in the conclusion to *Traité de métaphysique* in order to gain a first glimpse of the shape of this ambition. First, in the preface of the present book he says, "We are studying [in this book] some ideas: the idea of being, of the absolute, of transcendence, of space. We see that they carry us each time to something that is beyond ideas, or rather below them." The dialectic of reason reaches a point of failure, and in failing, it accomplishes itself by returning to the embodied world of things where it began. In the conclusion of the *Traité*, he says, therefore, "At the end of each of our meditations on the principal questions [of philosophy] we only reached out into the ineffable. Perhaps these different ineffables that we discovered each time should not be reduced to a unity, even though we must not exclude this possibility."[93] We ought not overly determine the ineffable, for in doing so we only evacuate its essential richness by papering it over with our abstractions.

The last words of both the preface and the *Traité* itself express all of this in an even clearer way. First, from the concluding lines of the *Traité*:

> Is it possible for us to return to immanence without losing transcendence? Can an eternal return of the dialect be conceived by which the first term, enriching and deepening itself, reappears in its primitive character? Is it demanded of the philosopher finally to transcend transcendence itself and to fall bravely back into immanence without leaving behind the value of his effort of transcendence?
>
> Questions of this kind are those that constitute philosophy itself, for philosophy is the attitude of questioning rather than the attitude of answers. It is the movement, obscurely perceived rather than seen, which goes from reality, through dialectic and antitheses, to ecstasy.[94]

And finally, the last lines of the preface. Here Wahl gives an express indication of the task to be undertaken in the present book:

> By returning to immanence, could we have lost transcendence? Can we preserve in myth that which thought destroys, that is, its essence, which gives it value? Could there be a return of dialectic, an eternal return by which the first term reappears enriched and impoverished? The following studies endeavor to give a response to this question. However, they themselves rather possess more of the character of questions than answers. At the least they place us in the presence of a movement that is glimpsed rather than seen and which strikes off from reality through a dialectic of antitheses and nonbeings in its struggle toward a mystery.[95]

These passages from these two texts are so similar that one might conclude that Wahl intends them as an essential statement of his philosophy. In honor of that, I let them stand in all of their poetic evocativeness and philosophical profundity without further comment.

What is the legacy of Jean Wahl? It is too early to tell. There has appeared to date no book-length study of the philosophical thought of Jean Wahl in its own right. In light of what we have examined above much could be said. Presently, however, I will draw this introduction to a close by attempting merely to express something from the perspective of at least one dimension of the philosophical vocation he so profoundly lived.

Among other things, Jean Wahl reminds us in a unique way, I think, that the history of Western civilization, and of world civilization itself, remains a story without an ending. If the dangers and risks have (already) changed dramatically since Wahl's time, the questions he was himself asking have only intensified. Wahl's approach to the questions, the human questions, is presented—almost aphoristically, improvisationally—in this little book. What Wahl thought about was the insoluble mystery of human existence; his thinking is an embrace of this insolubility and he offers a set of rather minimalist proposals about how to navigate this mystery, the miracle of ourselves, without reduction, *in a manner faithful to it*. Wahl's minimalism stems, I think, not only from his poetic sensibility, his strong, pressing awareness of the acute limits and partiality of all thought and every conceptualization, but also from the fact that he was in the first place a historian of philosophy.[96]

Wahl's works from the beginning evince a singular grasp of the history of Occidental thought from the pre-Socratics to Heidegger. With this grasp Wahl approached every philosopher as a contemporary, for they were *his* contemporaries, asking the basic human questions (in however diverging manners) and attempting to live a response to them that does them justice.[97] He could often rightly be accused of anachronism. But this was the risk he was willing to take in order to philosophize. This risk is itself an authentically philosophical risk, for only through undertaking it can one understand what philosophy is.

Wahl's thought is, in other words, an act of hope. As long, in fact, as there are living human beings on this good earth, hope will remain, and hope, as Wahl's friend Gabriel Marcel said, is itself the original motivating principle behind philosophical reflection—hope that we can in fact come to an understanding regarding what there is, who we are, and what it means to be good. Philosophy is rooted in a desire to know the truth of things and where we humans stand in relation to it. Jean Wahl grasped this task in a singular way, and he realized that the "desire to know" was a defining feature of humanity and the first measure of any philosophy.

The second measure, we could say, is the permanent dissatisfaction that this desire to know generates: all answers we can give are partial answers. They are always insufficient. This permanent insufficiency in every philosophical proposal generated in the history of thought is ultimately understood when it is interpreted as a key to the situation of human being. When this is not recognized to the degree that it ought to be, that is, fundamentally, then the would-be philosopher proposes facile answers to reality. But reality permits of no "facility"; reality can never be mastered, *especially* by conceptuality and abstraction. And yet every philosophical answer partakes of the facile to a greater or lesser degree; the work of the philosopher is never finished.

The third measure of philosophy is that the desire to know, inflamed by the recognition of its own tragic character as the manifestation of its essential truth, must be lived. Wahl understood this too. The modern recovery of the goal of a *bios theoretikos*, wherein the insoluble questions of the philosopher are recognized as the human questions, and a life lived in accordance with this recognition, was precisely the importance for Wahl of the thought of Kierkegaard, and, by extension, of "existential philosophy," with which he at least partially identified himself.

Wahl was of course a man of his time, which might at times make his thought seem a little provincial. But his enduring significance is not found in the way he is wed to his time, but rather in the way he lived out the philosophical vocation itself *in* his time, to the questions he posed *to* his time, in other words, in the philosophical authenticity that breathes in every page of his writings, and makes his thought come brilliantly alive every time it meets the same double attitude of philosophical desire and hope in a reader. *Human Existence and*

Transcendence is a means toward the enlivening of the flame of philosophy in us.

––––––––––

I will conclude with an anecdote. It seems right to do so in writing what has become, it appears, the first (more or less) extended introductory account in English of the philosophical significance of a man for whom, first, philosophical inquiry was as complex and singular as the persons who engaged in it; and for whom, second, such an irreducible plurality of philosophical experience joins the most quotidian with the most profound and thereby speaks the ineffable miracle of human existence. The May 12, 1945, issue of *The New Yorker* referenced above relates the story of how Jean Wahl as a young man discovered philosophy by discovering himself as a philosopher, wondering at the paradox of identity and difference through the experience of temporal change: "Wahl has been occupied with such [philosophical] considerations . . . ever since, as a boy of fifteen, he heard the call to philosophy while he was in the act of putting on his pants. The details of that occasion are still very clear to him. One moment he was standing in his room half-dressed, without any pants on, and the next moment he was fully clothed. The boy with his pants on, it occurred to him, could not be said to be the same person, in the philosophical sense, as the boy with the pants off."[98]

If one cannot "step into the same river twice," in the famous words of Heraclitus, something similar, Wahl teaches us, goes for our pants.

––––––––––

The work in your hands is an annotated translation of Wahl's 1944 *Existence humaine et transcendance* in its entirety and a commentary on his lecture to the Société française de philosophie, delivered on December 4, 1937. It is an introduction to the thought of one of the central figures in French philosophy and Parisian intellectual life of the last century. The present edition aims to make (or rather, to allow Wahl to make) a contribution to contemporary reflection by proposing—and enacting—the relevance of his "philosophy of transcendence" today.

By its publication I intend to help reopen the dossier on Jean Wahl the philosopher. Any annotation added to the text is clearly set apart from the original, and meant solely to magnify or contextualize a concept or theme. Departures from the original form of the French text are minimal and are explained in text and undertaken for the sake of producing the best English-language edition possible, I hope in fidelity to the spirit of the original. Wahl switches back and forth between the first person singular and plural in this text. It is sometimes odd, and yet not clearly an irregularity the translator should suppress. Perhaps it is a rhetorical strategy to focus the shared reflection of author and reader that he hopes to generate on the existential "I" that must feel the living weight, as it were, of philosophical ideas discussed. I therefore retained this distinctive usage in the translation. Translation from one language to another is a matter of the communication of "spirit," of which the "letter," though of course irreplaceable in itself, is still simply a vehicle. There is no "spirit" for material beings like ourselves without its incarnation in the "letter," but nevertheless these two are not for all that identified, as the very possibility of translation (and of all communication) severely demonstrates. Translator's notes are enclosed in brackets. The scholarly apparatus, including the introduction and appendices, is included as a means toward better understanding Jean Wahl, his world, and his thought—in the hope that they will serve the happenings of philosophy. Philosophy happens . . . but not apart from the awareness of how it has already happened. I hope readers will find my annotations of use to that end.

A debt of thanks is owed to my colleague Jeffrey Hanson for his translation of the letters, to Genevieve Fahey for proofreading the whole and for her suggestions for improving the translation, as well as to Margo Shearman, an extremely competent and judicious copyeditor. Thanks also to Barbara Wahl for helping me in an irreplaceable way at the very beginning of this project, especially for putting me in contact with Mme Laurence Gudin of Éditions Baconnière, the Swiss press that originally published Wahl's book and which continues the same august tradition of philosophical publication today. As the latter told me, often the best projects take the longest to materialize, at least much longer than was originally foreseen. On that note, it was my *Doktorvater* and colleague, Professor Kevin Hart, who originally suggested to me during those halcyon days of doctoral studies that this project was one worthy of pursuit, and I thank him and Jeffrey Bloechl for receiving this work in their book series, and for always keeping the path open.

W. C. H.

Melbourne, July 2014, and Paris, June 2015

NOTES

The epigraph is from the original French edition: Jean Wahl, *Existence humaine et transcendance* (Neuchâtel: Éditions de la Baconnière, 1944), 29n1.

1. "Subjectivité et transcendance," *Bulletin de la Société française de philosophie* 37, no. 5 (1937): 161–211.

2. See Emmanuel Levinas, "Jean Wahl: Sans avoir ni être," in the book collecting the keynote papers (by Levinas, Paul Ricoeur, and Xavier Tilliette) for a colloquium in Geneva in 1975 celebrating the legacies of Wahl and Gabriel Marcel, who died in 1974 and 1973, respectively: Emmanuel Levinas, Paul Ricoeur, and Xavier Tilliette, *Jean Wahl et Gabriel Marcel* (Paris: Beauchesne, 1976), 17. The introduction to this little book was composed by Jeanne Hersch, herself a participant in the meeting.

3. His massive Études *kierkegaardiennes* (Paris: F. Aubier, 1938) remains a classic.

4. *Le rôle de l'instant dans la philosophie de Descartes* (Paris: F. Alcan, 1920).

5. *Les philosophes pluralistes d'Angleterre et d'Amérique* (Paris: F. Alcan, 1920).

6. *Le malheur de la conscience dans la philosophie de Hegel* (Paris: Rieder, 1929). "One of the first signs of serious French interest in Hegel" (Gary Gutting, *French Philosophy in the Twentieth Century* [Cambridge: Cambridge University Press, 2001], 109).

7. See for this view Alan D. Schrift, *Twentieth Century French Philosophy: Key Themes and Thinkers* (Oxford: Wiley-Blackwell, 2006).

8. See Mathias Girel's introduction to the recent edition of Wahl's *Vers le concret* (1932; Paris: Vrin, 2013), 5–26.

9. *Totality and Infinity*, of course, is dedicated to Marcelle and Jean Wahl.

10. Emmanuel Levinas, *Totality and Infinity*, trans. Alfonso Lingis (Pittsburgh: Duquesne University Press, 1969), 35n2.

11. On Wahl's account of transcendence as a hermeneutic for the two major moments of Levinas's thought, see Roger Burggraeve, "Affected by the Face of the Other: The Levinasian Movement from the Exteriority to the Interiority of the

Infinite," *Dialegesthai. Revistia telematica di filosofia* 11 (2009). Online: http://mondodomani.org/dialegesthai/rbu01.

12. For further details of this narrative, see Hamilton Basso's article "Profiles: Philosopher: Jean Wahl," in *The New Yorker*, May 12, 1945, 27–41. Also of importance is Barbara Wahl's article-memoir "Autour de Jean Wahl: Textes, traces, témoignages," *Rivista di storia della filosofia* 3 (2011): 517–38.

13. For a thorough presentation of the significance of this historical moment, see the collection, *Artists, Intellectuals, and World War II: The Pontigny Encounters at Mount Holyoke College, 1942–1944*, ed. Christopher E. G. Benfey and Karen Remmler (Amherst: University of Massachusetts Press, 2006).

14. One should consult the appendix to Levinas, Ricoeur, and Tilliette, *Jean Wahl et Gabriel Marcel*, 89–92, for a biographical notice and bibliography of Wahl's major works compiled by his daughter.

15. If not of the intellectual traditions of all the classical civilizations of the world, Near Eastern, Indian, Chinese . . . See David Bentley Hart, *The Experience of God: Being, Consciousness, Bliss* (New Haven: Yale University Press, 2014), as well as Robert Bellah, *Religion in Human Evolution* (Cambridge, MA: Harvard University Press, 2011). Similarly, Gabriel Marcel speaks of "the spiritual tradition of humanity" in his contribution to the discussion at the meeting, recorded below.

16. *Traité de métaphysique* (Paris: Payot, 1953), 625. I will recall this remarkable quotation below, when I suggest that Wahl anticipates by several decades the defining moment of contemporary French phenomenology (viz., its "theological turn").

17. *Beyond Secular Order* (Oxford: Wiley, 2013), 19–20. These "certain modes of theology," according to Milbank's exemplification of a well-known genealogy of modernity, happen to be found in late medieval aberrations from classical Christian orthodoxy of some English Franciscan responses to the rediscovery of Aristotle, and then in even later (misled) interpretations of Thomas Aquinas in the Dominican and Jesuit commentarial tradition.

18. Aristotle quotes this in, e.g., *On the Soul* 411a 7–8. See also Pseudo-Aristotle, *On the Universe* 6, 397b 17–18. Wahl himself refers to it in *Poésie, pensée, perception* (Paris: Calmann-Lévy, 1948), 26, and *Traité de métaphysique*, 594–626.

19. Aristotle, *Metaphysics* A 982b 19; *The Complete Works of Aristotle*, vol. 2, ed. Jonathan Barnes (Princeton: Princeton University Press, 1984), 1554.

20. As an example see Xenophanes of Colophon's famous critique of anthropomorphism, B 23, 14 and 15 (Hermann Diels and Walther Kranz, *Die Fragmente der Vorsokratiker*, 10th ed. [Berlin: Weidmann, 1952]); See also Aristotle, *On the Universe* 6, "on the cause which holds all things together," 397b 10–401b 30.

21. See the *Theaetetus* 176a–b.

22. To allude to Pierre Hadot's breakthrough phrase. See *Exercices spirituels et philosophie antique* (Paris: Études augustiniennes, 1981).

23. It is worth seeing here Wahl's comments in the conclusion to *Traité de métaphysique* (718–19) summarizing his late chapters on God (IX.2) and on the multiple types of transcendence (perfection, infinity, unity, the absolute, the transcendent) which tend to be unified and focused on the divinity (IX.3). For Wahl the philosopher discovers the divine as the terminus of the tendency of reason to move toward a reduction of the multiple ineffables to a unity, but does not discover a final justification for that tendency; the dialectic of reason never comes to rest on the final term.

24. See Peter Koslowski's profound remarks on ancient Gnosticism, which, one must say, is a mode of thinking that applies (at least here) a glass of magnification (if also distortion) on an essential feature of human rationality: *Philosophien der Offenbarung* (Padderborn: Ferdinand Schöningh, 2001), 143–56.

25. For exploration of the endless evocative and tantalizing analogies across Greek, ancient Near Eastern, and Indian civilizations, see in particular Thomas McEvilley, *The Shape of Ancient Thought: Comparative Studies in Greek and Indian Philosophies* (New York: Allworth Press, 2012).

26. From this crucial perspective it is the later Schelling who recovers this attitude with the fullest force. See, for example, his *Lectures on the History of Modern Philosophy*, trans. Andrew Bowie (1836; Cambridge: Cambridge University Press, 1994).

27. One *can* argue that this is the teaching of Saint Paul, for whom the Cross, in revealing the "folly" of human wisdom, also redeems it: see Rom. 12:1–2 and 1 Cor. 1–3; for the fathers of the church see esp. Clement of Alexandria, *Stromata* I, 18, 90. For a general account of this see Hans Urs von Balthasar, "Philosophy, Christianity, Monasticism," *Explorations in Theology*, vol. 2: *Spouse of the Word* (San Francisco: Ignatius Press, 1991), 333–71.

28. See Augustine, *City of God* VIII, 10.

29. See Peter Struck, *Birth of the Symbol: Ancient Readers at the Limits of Their Texts* (Princeton: Princeton University Press, 2004), esp. chaps. 6, 7, and the epilogue, for late Neoplatonism and the enduring significance of this tradition.

30. See Hans-Dieter Gondek and Laszlo Tengelyi, *Neue Phänomenologie in Frankreich* (Berlin: Suhrkamp, 2011), for whom a defining feature of the "new phenomenology" is the direct result of a "turn" to religious phenomena, which has fundamentally transformed both the conception of the phenomenon and the phenomenological sensibility itself.

31. *Dis-Enclosure: The Deconstruction of Christianity*, vol. 1, trans. Bettina Bergo, Gabriel Malenfant, and Michael B. Smith (New York: Fordham University Press, 2008); *Adoration: The Deconstruction of Christianity*, vol. 2, trans. John McKeane (New York: Fordham University Press, 2012).

32. See for example Heidegger's famous comment in the Zürich Seminar, Nov. 6, 1951, in GA 15 436-f. "Faith has no need of the 'thought' of being," etc.

33. *Phenomenological Interpretation of Aristotle*, trans. Richard Rojcewicz (Bloomington: Indiana University Press, 2001), 148.

34. Ibid.

35. *Dis-Enclosure*, 1.

36. See esp. *Heidegger et la question de Dieu*, ed. Richard Kearney and Joseph O'Leary, 2nd ed. (Paris: Presses Universitaires de France, 2009).

37. See, for example, Jean-Luc Marion, "The Possible and Revelation," in *The Visible and the Revealed*, trans. Christina M. Gschwandtner (New York: Fordham University Press, 2008).

38. See Jean-Luc Marion's contribution to the debate mentioned immediately below.

39. See *God, the Gift, and Postmodernism*, ed. John Caputo and Michael Scanlon (Bloomington: Indiana University Press, 1999).

40. Published in *Dieu en tant que* Dieu: *La question philosophique*, ed. Philippe Capelle-Dumont (Paris: Cerf, 2012), 239–82.

41. The conclusion that "philosophy, reduced to what we control of it, is undertaken in the field of the possible and the question of the impossible becomes the central question of the limits of philosophy" (268) leads directly to the recognition that "there is no outside of the Christological question, not even under the regime of deconstruction" (282). With Christ we are "hors-texte," outside of any a priori determination of what we are doing in thought, even, ultimately the division of labor between discourses. Thinking after Christ, however, the distinction emerges between the two modalities of reason, theology and philosophy—never wholly identifiable but never wholly separable (see "On the Foundations of the Distinction between Theology and Philosophy," *Budhi* 13, no. 1–3 [2009], http://journals.ateneo.edu/ojs/index.php/budhi/issue/view/34).

42. Carl Schmitt, *Political Theology*, trans. George Schwab (Chicago: University of Chicago Press, 2006).

43. Ernst Kantorowicz, *The King's Two Bodies* (Princeton: Princeton University Press, 1997); Henri de Lubac, *Corpus Mysticum*, trans. Gemma Simmonds (Notre Dame, IN: University of Notre Dame Press, 2007).

44. See esp. his 1966 *The Legitimacy of the Modern Age*, trans. Robert M. Wallace (Cambridge, MA: MIT Press, 1985).

45. According to Franke ("Cosmopolitan Conviviality and Negative Theology: Europe's Vocation to Universalism," *Journal of European Studies* 44, no. 1 [2014]: 30–49), the present "vocation" of European thought is a "non-predicative universality" that creates a permanently open "space" for inclusive dialogue among religions and cultures which gives the ground of transcendence only by permanently withholding it in a paradoxical incommensurability. See also the introductory essays to his *On What Cannot Be Said*, 2 vols. (Notre Dame, IN: University of Notre Dame Press, 2007), and his most recent statement of his

position, *A Philosophy of the Unsayable* (Notre Dame, IN: University of Notre Dame Press, 2014).

46. Harry Austryn Wolfson, *The Philosophy of the Church Fathers*, vol. 1: *Faith, Trinity, Incarnation*, 3rd ed. (Cambridge, MA: Harvard University Press, 1970).

47. David Bentley Hart, *Atheist Delusions: The Christian Revolution and Its Fashionable Enemies* (New Haven: Yale University Press, 2009).

48. See on this my interview with Jean-François Courtine, in Tarek R. Dika and W. Chris Hackett, *Quiet Powers of the Possible: Interviews in Contemporary French Phenomenology* (New York: Fordham University Press, 2016).

49. See of course Dominique Janicaud et al., *Phenomenology and the "Theological Turn": The French Debate* (New York: Fordham University Press, 2000).

50. Jean-François Courtine, "Interview," in Dika and Hackett, *Quiet Powers of the Possible*.

51. Jean-Yves Lacoste, *La phénoménalité de Dieu: Neuf études* (Paris: Cerf, 2008); *From Theology to Theological Thinking*, trans. W. Chris Hackett (Charlottesville: University of Virginia Press, 2014).

52. Emmanuel Falque, *Passer le Rubicon: Philosophie et théologie: Essai sur les frontières* (Brussels: Lessius, 2013).

53. Jean-Luc Marion, *Certitudes négatives* (Paris: Grassette et Fasquelle, 2010).

54. See again Jean-Luc Marion, "On the Foundation of the Distinction between Theology and Philosophy," in *Certitudes*.

55. *Existence humaine et transcendance*, 113–24.

56. Short-sighted because it lacks the breadth and depth opened to the mind by the theological and religious.

57. See similarly Paul Ricoeur's concluding remarks, "Entre Gabriel Marcel et Jean Wahl," in *Jean Wahl et Gabriel Marcel*, 57–87.

58. This "project" is anticipated by the present volume in all of its major dimensions and developed particularly in *Traité de métaphysique* and especially his last and most original book, *Expérience métaphysique* (Paris: Flammarion, 1964).

59. See "Jean Wahl: Neither Having nor Being," 56.

60. Ibid.

61. I translate Barbara Wahl's transcription of this letter, "Autour de Jean Wahl," 527.

62. This interview was conducted around 1968 or 1969. He is referring to his book composed in the United States, written in English, *The Philosopher's Way* (Oxford: Oxford University Press, 1948). Barbara Wahl, "Autour de Jean Wahl," 531.

63. See, for example, Saint Thomas Aquinas, *Summa theologica*, I 12, 12 resp., and 13, 1 resp.

64. *Poems* (1945), 164. Quoted in Barbara Wahl, "Autour de Jean Wahl," 527n21.

65. Wahl was born into an "assimilated" and nonpracticing Jewish family; he married a Catholic, and his children were raised in the Catholic Church. See Barbara Wahl's irreplaceable article for research into the existential complexity of Wahl's thought in an intimate and moving presentation in homage to her father.

66. Barbara Wahl, "Autour de Jean Wahl," 528.

67. Ibid., 536.

68. *Études kierkegaardiennes*, chap. 7, 210–55. See Samuel Moyn, "Transcendence, Morality and History: Emmanuel Levinas and the Discovery of Kierkegaard in France," *Yale French Studies* 104 (2004): 22–54. This passage is discussed on p. 40.

69. See esp. his closing remarks, which introduce, by reference to Nicolai Hartmann, the distinction between transcendence as movement and transcendence as term, which the dynamic character of the first distinction allows us to see more clearly.

70. See also the penultimate paragraph of the conclusion, which conceives of this "return to immanence without losing transcendence" as among the "constitutive questions of philosophy itself" (721–72).

71. Lee Braver, "A Brief History of Continental Realism," *Continental Philosophy Review* 45 (2012): 261–89.

72. The classic statement of this in the context of an "overcoming" of the ontological difference, or, in Marion's words, of the "liberation of being," can be found in his *God without Being*, trans. Thomas A. Carlson (Chicago: University of Chicago Press, 1991), 53–107, which proposes a "difference more essential to being than ontological difference itself" (85).

73. See, again, the quotation from *Traité de métaphysique*, 625, translated above.

74. *Traité de métaphysique*, 602.

75. This is the famous definition of phenomenology presented in *Being and Time* § 7, trans. Joan Stambaugh (Albany: SUNY Press, 1996), 30.

76. "Subjectivité et transcendance," 195.

77. Ibid.

78. For Heidegger, Kierkegaard "got the farthest" in the theological interpretation of anxiety, but remained within the theological domain for which the ontic and ontological registers were never appropriately distinguished. See *Being and Time*, n4, to §40, 190 (Stambaugh translation, 178, note on pp. 404–5).

79. This, for Kierkegaard of course, is all accomplished in the concrete figure of Christ.

80. I use this phrase in order to gesture pointedly toward Jean-Yves Lacoste's small masterpiece, *Experience and the Absolute: Disputed Questions on the*

Humanity of Man, trans. Mark Raftery-Skehan (New York: Fordham University Press, 2004).

81. *Étude sur le "Parménide" de Platon* (Paris: Rieder, 1930): the importance of which, however, has yet to be appropriately manifest . . .

82. *Traité de métaphysique*, 619.

83. *Unfading Light*, trans. Thomas Allan Smith (Grand Rapids, MI: Eerdmans, 2012), 104 (emphasis mine). Or again: "The object of religion, God, is something that on the one hand is completely transcendent, of a different nature, and external to the world and the human being, but on the other hand is revealed to religious consciousness, touches it, enters inside it, becomes its immanent content. Both moments of religious consciousness are given simultaneously, like poles, in their mutual repulsion and attraction. The object of religion is something transcendent-immanent or immanent-transcendent according to its essence" (103).

84. *Traité de métaphysique*, 619. The last expression comes from the New Testament (Acts 17:28), wherein Luke's Saint Paul quotes a pagan poet, Epimenides.

85. Ibid.

86. It is interesting, and would prove a fascinating study auxiliary to this one, that the great mystical literature of Christianity is filled with ways of addressing this very question (think of the instructions for "testing the spirits" in Teresa of Avila or John of the Cross).

87. Adorno's critique is found primarily in two book reviews of Wahl's *Études kierkegaardiennes*, the first in *Journal of Philosophy* 36, no. 1 (1939): 18–19; the second in *Studies in Philosophy and Social Science* 8, no. 1–2 (1939–40): 232–33. See the discussion of Adorno's critique of Wahl and their correspondence in Jon Stewart, *Kierkegaard's Influence on Philosophy: German and Scandinavian Philosophy* (Aldershot: Ashgate, 2012), 22–24.

88. See Samuel Moyn's discussion of this intra-Jewish debate about the interpretation of Kierkegaard in "Transcendence, Morality and History," 40–42.

89. In the interview discussed above, in response to the question "What do you think of someone who converts?" Wahl says candidly, "But I interrogate myself [*je m'interroge*]. I tell myself that I will not convert. I tell myself that I am not converted. I often find myself thinking about Bergson who is . . . who had taken a position so complex that he wrote in his Testament: I believe that Catholicism is true! And yet he was not baptized—in order, he said, not to separate himself from those who would probably be persecuted" (Barbara Wahl, "Autour de Jean Wahl," 532).

90. This tension is, again, well presented by Barbara Wahl in her article.

91. "Subjectivité et transcendance," 195.

92. *Traité de métaphysique*, 646.

93. Ibid., 718–19.

94. Ibid., 721.

95. *Existence humaine et transcendance*, 24–25.

96. See Emmanuel Levinas's remarks in "Jean Wahl, Neither Having nor Being," in *Outside the Subject*, trans. Michael B. Smith (London: Continuum, 1993), 51–64, esp. 53–54.

97. This approach is on full display in *The Philosopher's Way* and *Traité de métaphysique*.

98. "Profiles: Philosopher: Jean Wahl," 27–28.

HUMAN EXISTENCE
AND TRANSCENDENCE

Preface

It is perhaps not totally precise—although the observation wears well and should give us pause—to say after Jaspers that a new kind (do I say a new "race"?) of thinker was formed in the nineteenth century, that of the poet-thinker, Nietzsche and Kierkegaard. It is not totally precise because Pascal, Lucretius, perhaps Dante—to set aside names even more ancient—are equally poet-thinkers. And it is also not totally precise anymore to say that the philosophy of existence was born in the nineteenth century. Pascal is the ever-living refutation of such a judgment. And is not the philosophy of Plato directly tied to the meditation of an existing being named Plato on two existing beings named Plato and Socrates? Plato's philosophy is a reflection on the life, condemnation, and death of Socrates.

The fact no less remains that the borders of philosophy dissolved in this milieu at the end of the nineteenth century, as have also in a lesser way borders of every kind. There are no longer many pure painters (if there ever have been any). Courbet or Manet were perhaps the last great painters. Van Gogh and Cézanne are something else entirely. What thinker before Kierkegaard had taken as the center of his meditation his own most personal experience and his own history? To find some analogues, we would have to turn to poets like Nerval or Rimbaud.

But it is not only the fact that Nietzsche and Kierkegaard are poet-thinkers,[1] nor even that they have common adversaries (the historian and the professor of philosophy), nor even that before the unity of monism they raise up the unicity of both the Unique and of the Overman;[2] and it is not only because they oppose philosophical reflection, one, with belief, the other, with the will to power[3]—it is not simply these reasons that explain the profound kinship, the coincidence of opposites, that unite Kierkegaard and Nietzsche. Beginning with the observation, God is dead—which they take in opposite senses (for one, the death of God is the death of a God who is revealed to be God by his death, and which is our salvation; for the other, our salvation is the death of God, of a God who by his death ceases to be God)— they pursue their meditation, hunting for eternity in the instant: for Kierkegaard in the instant of repetition and resurrection, lived by the Unique, for Nietzsche in the instant of the eternal return, lived by the Overman. The Nietzschean instant as much as the Kierkegaardian instant is the fusion of what Heidegger will call the three ecstasies of time, within what he will call (and on this point his meditation only continues that of Nietzsche and Kierkegaard) the resoluteness of decision.

One proposes an immanence capable of overwhelming us as much as transcendence does, if we allow ourselves to be overwhelmed; the

---

1. I note also that both Nietzsche and Kierkegaard doubt at the same time that they affirm, and know at the same time that they doubt. For them it is less a matter of dogmatic affirmations than of passion and will (see on this point what Jaspers writes about Nietzsche).

Both have made problems of themselves. And in such a way that one would have to study the relation between the poet-thinkers and "problematic" men, between poetry and doubt.

2. It is in this sense that Löwith said that Hegel is the last great philosopher.

3. It would be interesting to follow the struggle of philosophers at the end of the nineteenth century and of those of the twentieth century against the *philosophia perennis*, who perhaps now know that it is mortal (like the civilizations of which Valéry spoke): the struggle against Plato, against a certain conception of Plato, in my opinion false, carried out by Nietzsche, Kierkegaard, Bergson, James, Heidegger; the struggle against Descartes, waged above all by Heidegger and Jaspers; against Spinoza (James); and against Leibniz (Russell).

other proposes a transcendence that terrifies and consoles us. Both place man before an abyss; and it is within a hairsbreadth of his downfall, in anguish and heartbreak, that he is revived and starts anew.

Through the paradoxes before which they find themselves (the birth and death of God, the eternal return), through the paradoxes that they feel in themselves and that they are in themselves, through living their discordances, the Kierkegaardian Unique and the Nietzschean Overman intensify their individuality.

Starting from this point Nietzsche and Kierkegaard construct their existential dialectic, starting from here they forge their personalities as a union of opposites and—to recall the ancient phrase of Heraclitus—a harmony of strife. They are a living, felt dialectic, not a dialectic that goes from thesis to antithesis and then to synthesis, but a dialectic that from a thesis goes to a thesis and an antithesis, in order then to go toward a thesis that is not posed, that cannot be posed, and which is like the disappearance of consciousness in the ecstasy at Sils Maria[4] or in religious meditation.[5]

By contrast to the Hegelian dialectic (thesis-antithesis-synthesis), and even to the Platonic dialectic (ascending dialectic, contemplation, descending dialectic), we could imagine an existential dialectic that would go from presence to dialectic, and from dialectic to ecstasy through the play of antitheses that destroy each other in order to cede their place to this ecstasy. From the ecstasy of perception (positive ontology) to the ecstasy of mystery (negative ontology), from the plenitude of the real to the apparent vacuity of surreal being, one passes

4. [A town in Switzerland where Nietzsche spent the summers of 1881 and 1883–88.]

5. The contradictions of Nietzsche, Jaspers tells us, ought to orient us each time to an unsayable center by means of their relation to what gives them their depth of meaning.

The thought of the eternal return is destructive and constructive: destructive inasmuch as it affirms the absurd, and constructive inasmuch as it reaffirms being, establishing the infinite value of the instant. Nietzsche's art consists of making the greatest dissatisfaction into the greatest satisfaction, of the becoming absurd into an accomplished being made up of divine instants, of decadence into the gate that leads to the richest and most self-assured of cultures.

through this dialectic, this coming and going of thought and ripping apart of antitheses.

Short dialectical chains between two moments where the dialogue ceases—at least the apparent dialogue—in order to leave the word, if I can put it this way, to silence. A silence of perception through which the spirit is nourished by things, a silence of ecstasy where it merges with the highest point of itself and the world.

Between the two, this tension, this intensity that defines existence placed between the transcendent immanence of perception and the immanent transcendence of ecstasy.

These last words show us that even in these moments where the dialogue ceases, it continues, that as soon as reflection is attached to them, there is a dialectic both of perception and ecstasy.[6]

We find this tension between antitheses at every moment—when we take the idea of being that divides into its objective and subjective aspects, into resistance and completion, into independence and communion, or when we take the idea of the absolute that divides into a transcendent absolute and an immanent absolute, into the absolute of Damascius and the absolute of Bradley, into discord and immersion, division and union. If there is a truth that seems to emerge from these studies, it is the truth of the unsayable, out of which discourse begins, to which it returns, without this being the same unsayable from which it escapes and to which it goes.

The Hegelian dialectic leads to the vision of a totality. The same goes for the Platonic dialectic. The dialectic that we foresee remains partial and comes from a logic of quality where the most is not more than the least, and which, occasionally, may orient us, not toward a richer view of the universe, but toward a more naked contact with certain parts of the universe, with those tiny particulars of which Blake spoke and about which Nietzsche thought.

6. Plato, Damascius, Hegel, and Kierkegaard have been able to make us feel this quasi-ineffable junction of relation and nonrelation, of immanence and transcendence. The absolute is given in its relation with the subjective and yet can never be given in this relation. This situation is also that of the person and even of the thing.

The ineffable that we will reach could be expressed in the plural; there will be *ineffables*, multiple ones, each infinite, limited-unlimited realities. The absolute is not the totality (in any case, not the totality that would be an all-encompassing aggregation). It is intensity or density. For me it is a matter of a felt absolute [*un absolu senti*], and which can be felt in every little thing.

———————

Rarely can one so strongly see the immanent dialectic at work in systems than in contemporary thought as it unfolds: the idealism of Royce somehow summons forth the neo-Realism of Perry, and neo-Realism summons forth a realism of a totally different, and opposed, sort, that of Strong and Santayana. Husserl: who prefigures in his philosophy the being-in-the-world of Heidegger, who shows us present objects so well, out there, in their corporeity, who so strongly characterizes the natural point of view, who insists on the necessity of perception as the starting point and end point for science, who, in my opinion, shatters the nonintentionality of perception (perception is not a sign; it is; this is the Husserlian equivalent of the Bergsonian theory of the image), who emphasizes the role of the body, without, for all that (unfortunately it seems to me), abandoning idealist presuppositions, and who makes us see not only a world of essences but a world of values—yet Husserl wants to bracket the sensible world, to separate essence and existence, to define essence. A vain task. The thinking he provoked has developed far beyond his own thought. Heidegger shows that the world cannot be bracketed, that existence has no essence, that the idea of essence is artificial, in the most proper sense of the term, modeled on human artifice, modeled on the model seen by the craftsman.[7]

———————

7. I emphasize that one will find in *Arbalète*, vols. 3–4, a clear and faithful translation (as clear as possible) of some passages from Heidegger. I cannot recommend with the same enthusiasm the translation of Corbin, which was published by Gallimard in the collection *Les essais*. Despite all the very great qualities of this translator (in different realms of thought he has given us works of value), and despite his often deep enthusiasm, the translation leaves something to be desired. His intuitions sometimes deceive him.

Thus by a more objective observation we find again the path of the dialectic that we had glimpsed. But the path does not explain itself; it demands that it be placed between its starting point and end point.

————————

Before putting the path back in its place in this way, it is appropriate to note that if with Nietzsche and Heidegger human thought has come to pose subjectivity in its most intense state, although both pose at the same time an object that by contact with which subjectivity is sharpened (an object-subject in Kierkegaard, since it is God incarnate; an object without reason, which is the eternal return, in Nietzsche), then, on the other hand, in Whitehead and Heidegger the object, the thing, is perceived in its most profound being, though one is guided by his insistence on being-in-the-world, the other by his insistence on the world of causal efficacy. Man, says Heidegger, is naturally outside of himself. Man is always with other men and near things; this *near* and *with* are intimately tied together. And it is this fact that man is outside of himself that constitutes transcendence such as Heidegger conceives it in his world where the transcendence of the traditional God no longer subsists.[8]

This is not to say, however, that Whitehead and Heidegger turn their noses up at this subjective thought, the force of which we have seen in Nietzsche and Kierkegaard. In order to sense their affinities with the poetic vision of things it is sufficient to reflect on the way that Whitehead likes to cite Wordsworth and Shelley and that Heidegger likes to cite Hölderlin and Rilke.

Heidegger and Whitehead place us in the presence of the world of objects. At the same time Whitehead liberates us from classical

8. Heidegger has equally emphasised very well the notion of philosophy as return to a trusting or confident relation with things. Giving himself over to a somewhat adventurous etymology, he says that being a philosopher means being familiar with things like a friend even more than having friendship with wisdom. The philosopher is the one who finds the profound union of human being with being (Lecture Course of 1928–29 [*Einleitung in die Philosophie*, GA 27], lectures 2, 7, and 16). It is this that he still conveys by the idea that *Dasein* is Being-in-the-world; it constitutes a world, starting from which it understands itself.

conceptions of time and space; no one, not even Eddington or de Broglie, whose reflections go so far, not even Bergson, has better shown the necessity of breaking with the spatio-temporal schemes of classical thought, of conceiving the jumble and effulgence of phenomena in such a way that *here* and *now* no longer have any meaning. Here Hegel's critique, perhaps merely verbal at root, is extended; for it is no longer the terms *here* and *now* that are critiqued, but the very idea of a *here* and *now*.

The universe that modern science presents us with is made of relations at once more massive and subtler, more shapeless, vaster, and more nuanced than those that classical science used. When we have to connect the phenomena, the idea of causality, too crude and simplistic, cannot satisfy us.[9]

———————

Nothing is more characteristic of contemporary philosophy than this emphasis on the most subjective of the subjective and the most objective of the objective (with this reservation that this word "objective" expresses very poorly this perceived density behind concepts, this opacity, this entanglement without name and without corresponding idea, something like a primordial slime which refuses every idea, and about which perhaps Parmenides was thinking when he interrogated the young Socrates in Plato's dialogue).

In other activities we equally discover these loaded antitheses that appear at the apex of modern thought, this grand objectivism and grand subjectivism (to employ Sheldon's terms, who, it is true, applies them to other doctrines). We discover them among the highest activities of man, in other visions, like those of Van Gogh and Cézanne. Van Gogh, along with El Greco, represents subjectivity at its highest power, and Cézanne represents at its greatest intensity the need, the

———————

9. Heidegger says that science sees today that it is surrounded by something that as science it needs but that it can neither understand nor conceive. It is running up against its limits. Something "other" supports science and yet cannot be known by it (Lecture Course of 1928–29 [*Einleitung in die Philosophie*, GA 27], lectures 4 and 5.

hunger and thirst, for objectivity, and the need to "create the image" [*faire l'image*].[10]

Yet here we cannot separate grand objectivism and grand subjectivism. For destiny, a rational destiny like any destiny, says Hegel, demands that what we find in Cézanne is yet more than mere objectivity: a need for objectivity is something very subjective, appearing all the more subjective as we conceive it as attempted rather than as accomplished. And on the other side, Van Gogh knows—knows without knowing it—how to be engrossed in yellow and scarlet, and how to become every object.

Thus the subjective returns to the objective, just as the objective returned us to the subjective.

Perhaps this is an indication that, although it is important to push both sides as far as possible, they cannot be thought apart and even ought to be annihilated in the movement of thought as it attempts to attain to things.

We therefore find here dialectic and realism. We can observe the profound links that unite them. There is a dialectic of realism, extremely visible as we have seen in the history of its latest forms passing from the neo-Realism of Perry, a realist monism that allows for the identity of the object and its representation, to the critical realism of Strong, Santayana, and Sellars, who keep them separate. For the mind nothing is more difficult in fact (though this is no argument against this position) than to limit itself to a realist monism analogous to the theses of Bergson on the first page of *Matter and Memory* or to those of James in his famous article "Does 'Consciousness' Exist?" They want to stop short of this dialectic. Without doubt they are right. But the reason of the intellect does not know this reason of reason or experience the need ceaselessly to traverse anew the circle of oppositions and fusions of image and object.

10. [Wahl uses this expression attributed to Cézanne twice; I find it totally untranslatable. The verb *faire* has a thick layer of possible meanings. Here Wahl, following Cézanne, wants to express the creative power of the artist but more importantly, I think, the paradoxical originality of the image itself.]

If there is a dialectic of realism, this is because dialectic is not the explanatory term, or is such only because it is itself explained by the reality. Where does this play of antitheses come from, this mental play of conceits that makes contraries shine forth in the face of contraries, if not from this need it has to approach the real, a real that refuses all purely intellectual contact, which does not allow itself to be closed off and on which we could never have anything but successive, contradictory, and alternative perspectives, as Montherlant said?

We have already seen that dialectic will only be truly dialectical if it itself becomes dialecticized, by which we mean that the dialectic that makes each thing take place, should itself take place, and take place, in fact, between two nondialectical terms.[11]

---

11. This leads me to say that the theory of knowledge does not come first: it *is* not, for it presupposes a theory of reality. Doubtlessly, the theory of reality presupposes a theory of knowledge. There is a necessary circle of these two theories. But while the theory of reality does not hide from the demand for a theory of knowledge, the theory of knowledge hides from the demand for a theory of reality. The way that the theory of reality operates, therefore, is more straightforward. In the second place we could say—and Nicolai Hartmann felt this idea strongly—that at the very point where the theory of reality opens its eyes, the theory of knowledge takes things at a slant, squinting while observing the shimmering reflections of reflection. See equally Heidegger, Lecture Course of 1928–29 [*Einleitung in die Philosophie*, GA 27], lecture 15.

In particular, all the theories of knowledge founded on the idea of a subject standing over-against an object should be thoroughly reworked. As Heidegger said, "Some think that with the theory of the subject-object relation they have a fitting point of departure. Instead, they have closed the path that leads to a solution of the ontological problem." Between the subject and object there is an intimate union, in relation to which the theory of prehension in Whitehead, co-presence in Alexander, knowledge (in the Claudelian sense) in Claudel, attract our attention, at the same time as knowledge no longer appears as anything but the particular case of a more general relation. On this latter point we could refer to the efforts of Holt and Montague. For Holt consciousness is a cross section, for Bergson it is a cross section and a selection. Here we have an ingenious and important effort to determine consciousness from the starting point of something other than it. This attempt was a paradox, rarely attempted with so much consequence as at the end of the nineteenth and beginning of the twentieth centuries.

This can become an opportunity for us to take a look at the point of departure of dialectic, then at its point of arrival, at the reality of perception, and at the moment of ecstasy and mystery, the moment of transcendence.

———

The weakness of empiricism and realism is demonstrated in the fact that they have handed over to idealism the great admiration that comes along with lofty thought and demanding reflection.[12] From the starting point of the Kantian affirmation that being is position, we could pass to a positive philosophy analogous to Schelling and to the highest

———

We can fruitfully read Heidegger's critique of bad subjectivity (Lecture Course of 1928–29 [*Einleitung in die Philosophie*, GA 27], lectures 7, 10, and 15): "Philosophers have established subjectivity at too low a level."

We have already spoken above of the inadequacy of the concepts of the objective and subjective. In relation to this we cite here the passage in Heidegger who follows Husserl on this point more than he thinks, showing the inadequacy of the concepts of the objective and subjective to characterize intentionality: "Intentionality is neither objective, extant like an object, nor subjective in the sense of something that occurs within a so-called subject. Intentionality is neither objective nor subjective in the usual sense, although it is certainly both, but in a much more original sense, since intentionality, as belonging to *Dasein*'s existence, makes it possible that this being, the *Dasein*, comports existingly toward the extant . . . For the *Dasein* there is no outside, for which reason it is also absurd to talk about an inside. . . . Perceivedness is a qualification which pertains to the object without being objective, and to the subject without being subjective" [*Basic Problems of Phenomenology*, trans. Albert Hofstadter (Bloomington: Indiana University Press, 1982), 65, 66, 69].

Generally speaking, classical philosophy over-isolated its notion of intentionality. As Plato saw, every logos is a logos of something. From Aristotle to Hegel, every philosophy has left too far to the side the character of designation and judgment, what Heidegger calls its apophantic character.

Moreover, moved by a kind of pride, the idealist only wants to see the active element of perception, and even more so of judgment. But in both of these there is as much passivity as activity. As Heidegger said, the one who perceives surrenders himself to things and lets the things surrender themselves (Lecture Course of 1928–29 [*Einleitung in die Philosophie*, GA 27]).

12. Heidegger said that one could not even say that realism is not tenable since it has not penetrated into the realm of the philosophical problematic.

empiricism. In this way we could have a transcendental empiricism, as Schelling demonstrated, seeking the conditions by which experience is not merely possible but real, and this realism would be founded on the critique of the idea of the possible and on the reality of contingency (which goes hand in hand with the contingency of the necessary).[13] We could also have a radical empiricism, as James demonstrated,

13. Nietzsche's philosophy passed through different periods: a philosophy of illusion, a positivist period, and a Dionysiac period. If we left the second period in the background, nevertheless it ought not to be neglected. Philosophy as hammer was forged through this second period when principal philosophical concepts were critiqued as rarely as they ever have been. In Bergsonian philosophy we can find a positivism that is no less penetrating and destructive. We see such positivism in the critiques of the ideas of nothing, disorder, and the possible. Some of the affirmations of this negative philosophy, of this "positivism" that could be equally inspired by Nietzsche or Bergson, are: the primacy of the modality of reality over all others (mostly well discerned by Kant, but neglected, it seems, by the existentialists), the superiority of the pseudonegative over the pseudopositive (unknown by classical philosophy when it accorded a privilege to the perfect and the infinite over the imperfect and the finite). Something similar could be said about the idea that all knowledge, all truth, is retrospective.

It is finally Heidegger who will give some invaluable indications for the sake of this *destructio philosophorum*, at least in relation to the philosophers of the *philosophia perennis*, and toward a *philosophia actualis*, real and in act. Since the Greeks, philosophy has been oriented by the *logos*, which expresses, and the *eidos*, which is essentially expressible, the form inasmuch as it is expressible. Man, the being who speaks and sees, develops a world of words and spectacles. Yet the real world is not one of propositions and perspectives. This world of words and spectacles has been modeled on perception and production; everything is imagined under the form of the produced and the perceived. These two ideas are linked: that which is produced is first produced according to a model that is perceived. It is secondly perceived as independent. From there arises the distinction between essence and existence, form and matter. And from there the idea of an intellectual intuition, which Kant reserves for the Creator alone. But these schemes of production and the empirical (here the critique of Heidegger meets that of Brunschvicg) do not suffice: production presupposes the nonproduced, and this suggests the idea of matter. In the second place, there are some cases where the scheme of production just does not apply. This is precisely the case with the human being, which has no essence, no quiddity. It is not a *quid*, but a *quis*, a someone and not a something. It repels every application to itself of the distinction between essence and existence.

hospitable to both relations and terms, or an empiricism hospitable to essences, such as is found in G. E. Moore, Russell, and Husserl, or, finally, an affective empiricism, of which Bergsonian philosophy is the living proof.[14] Transcendental, radical, nonintellectual (these three empiricisms are inseparable): *this empiricism* is very far removed from what is offered in the classroom. It would allow us to bring together Pascal, Schelling and Hume, Russell, Boutroux and Scheler, Bergson, Nietzsche and Rauh.

Such an empiricism allows us to bring together a theory of contingency and a theory of reality.

This empiricism naturally leads to realism. Reflection only exists as reflection on that which is nonthought; consciousness only exists if there is nonconsciousness. Before my thought emerges, there is always something there. I think, therefore something is thought, which my thought is not. This apothegm is as true as the "I think therefore I am."[15]

14. We could conceive of an empiricism founded on internal observation that allows for existential theories of space and time and attempts to explain time by anticipation, memory, hope, fear, regret, and remorse. On the other hand, external observation allows us to say that time is not, space is not: whatever is, inasmuch as this word has meaning, are the things before and after, things in time. It is from abstraction, based on what we can call common things [*choses courantes*] rather than the course of events [*cours de choses*], that composes the idea of time, just as juxtaposed things, or things placed behind [*arrière-posées*] or before [*devant-posées*], compose the idea of space. Of course, to an idealist, what we are saying only forms a vicious circle.

15. This idea of the "always already," of the preliminary, plays a great role in Heidegger. In order for truth to have any meaning, it is necessary that man has always already a path of access to things. Excuse the barbarity of the expression: where there is knowledge, there is always a "setting up shop" beside that which we know. Every intentional relation has a specific understanding of the being to which it is related. This means that there is always already something unveiled.

But this idea of the preliminary is essential to the very definition of the truth: the truth uncovers the being as what it was independent of the fact of being uncovered or not.

Thus, from the idea of intentionality, Heidegger moves to that of a comprehension of the being of the being for which being is a concern, a variable comprehension following beings, and from this comprehension of the being of the being he moves to the idea of a preliminary moving among things.

Even more, systems of meaning are created, and not only by the mind. If, as Plato said, the eye is of the same kind as the sun, then for this empiricism as for Plato the light has formed it. Matter gives form to the form before the form informs matter, and a similar idea is found at the root of the conception of emergence in Alexander.

Novalis spoke of a magical idealism. Continuing a tradition that comes from Albert the Great and some Arab philosophers more than Aristotle and Plato, he profoundly tied together idealism and magic. But it is no less legitimate to attempt to construct a magical realism. Reid approached this when he spoke of a magic of perception.

Idealism-realism: it is true that these terms are hardly satisfying. And doubtlessly we should observe that absolute realism and absolute idealism come to be confused, to coincide; or, more precisely, it is *beyond* realism and idealism, or even more precisely, *below* them, that we should place ourselves, and even live out, the negation of all these -isms, which are only various points of view on that which cannot be perceived by vision.

In this way we approach a mysticism, but a mysticism of the thing and of the object before it is a mysticism of the person.

The realism of which we have spoken will not be a flat realism. Remaining at the level of our perception, not pulling apart this perception in accordance with something other than it, it will present us with artificially nonconcrete concrete realities, albeit born from a natural concrescence of things.

The thing! Rilke created a poetry of things, and Husserl made all the aspects of these things shine forth that are never given except in perspective and in adumbration. He makes present to us the luminosity of things that are given and which are not given. Never better than in modern thought has the thing been known in its multicolored perspectives as also in its opacity and invisibility. To take back up an idea that could characterize certain of Whitehead's conceptions, immanent

---

Said in yet another way, what is given thematically is first given non-thematically.

Or: *Dasein*, human being, always understands itself starting from a world that constitutes it.

and transcendent (or more accurately even equally eluding these two qualifications) are organizational ends.

———————

Once we have felt the presence of perception, the point of departure for the dialectic, we can envisage its point of arrival situated beyond consciousness, as perception was situated below it. In fact the dialectic of which we spoke implies distance, rupture,[16] estrangement, consciousness. Consciousness is always distance. As soon as there is consciousness there is a gulf to cross between it and reality that will never be crossed.

This shows thereby that even if the truth lies in judgment, reality lies in the realm of nonconsciousness. Here we are studying some ideas: the idea of being, of the absolute, of transcendence, of space. We see that they carry us each time to something that is beyond ideas, or rather, below them.

This also shows that every relation ought to be broken, founded on this transrelational experience, which is the true experience, non-experienced experience. This equally shows that it is in feeling [le sentiment] more than in reason that we find the most precise approximation of the absolute.

This finally shows that if we want to get back to paradise lost, we must lose ourselves in paradise regained; this is a condition for finding it. Consciousness occurs between this loss and rediscovery: consciousness is necessarily unhappy.

From its starting point to its end point, it passes through negativity, which leads the play of antitheses. But beyond this negativity there dwells an even more essential negativity, all-denying, destructive, and no longer merely negative, a need to annihilate its own thought in an attitude of submission to this domination by transcendence felt by the being.[17]

16. Not only regarding the relation between judgment and its object, but also within judgment itself, Bradley has admirably demonstrated this tearing apart and fragmentation.

17. The idea of a negative ontology should not lead us to believe in an objective nothingness. As Bosanquet has said, thought can only be thought with a content. It is therefore the feeling before being (I use this word because a better one

And if I can reach it, it is a living wall.

In this movement of transcendence there is an accomplishment of the
self that is at the same time a self-destruction, a failure that is also a
triumph. Phaëthon and Empedocles are fulfilled through destroying
themselves.[18]

Doubtlessly, what we can call the charm of these ideas of transcendence and the absolute derives from their ambiguity, from the sudden
flash of their meaning. Transcendence is both a movement toward and
a stable end; the absolute is the separating and the uniting. No one
has better highlighted this ambiguity than Plato in the *Parmenides*.
The first hypothesis is the separated absolute; the second is the uniting
absolute; and without a doubt, the uniting absolute ought to encompass the separated absolute—or at least ought to if the separated absolute allows it. Plato escapes these difficulties by erecting a theory of the
limit and the unlimited—or at least gives the appearance of escaping
them in this way. But the last line of the *Parmenides* shows us that they
remain by putting us in the presence of the unsayable.[19]

Thus, despite these ambiguities, the absolute and the transcendent preserve their value for thinking. They mark the extreme point
of thinking's effort, where thinking reaches its limit. And by this
limit, at this frontier, a light begins to shimmer about which we cannot say whether it comes from thought, from the Other or from the
nameless Thing.

The same can be said for the concept of the instant. Since Plato it
has haunted the minds of philosophers and writers. From the instant of

---

does not exist) which is negative; but everything thought is objective, and the
negative is so more than anything else.

18. [The demigod Phaëthon (as Ovid tells the story) sought to drive his father
Phoebus's sun-chariot but lost control and was struck by a thunderbolt to save the
earth. Empedocles was said to have cast himself into the volcanic fires of Mount
Etna as an apotheosis.]

19. ["Whether one is or is not, it and the others both are and are not, and
both appear and do not appear all things in all ways, both in relation to themselves
and each other" (*Parmenides* 166c, in *Plato: Complete Works*, ed. John M. Cooper
[Indianapolis: Hackett, 1997], 397.)]

the third hypothesis to the instantaneous pleasure of Aristippus, taken back up by Walter Pater and André Gide, to the theological instant (the instant of Incarnation, of resurrection, of last judgment *in ictu oculi*) to Kierkegaard's iteration of it, and then Dostoyevsky's, to the Nietzschean eternal return that sanctifies the instant, to Rimbaud's eternity, we would have to follow these meditations as they unfold from the [primal] search for lost eternity, rediscovered in the instant, and to ask if the instant is not for the modern thinker a consoling myth more than a reality, a cheap imitation of eternity, and yet at the same time a reality, an existential reality ceaselessly offered, ceaselessly lost.

By returning to immanence, could we have lost transcendence? Can we preserve in myth that which thought destroys, that is, its essence, which gives it value? Could there be a return of dialectic, an eternal return by which the first term reappears enriched and impoverished? The following studies endeavor to give a response to this question. However, they themselves rather possess more of the character of questions than answers. At the least they place us in the presence of a movement that is glimpsed rather than seen and which strikes off from reality through a dialectic of antitheses and nonbeings in its struggle toward a mystery.

On Existence

The idea of existence is manifold. In the language of Aristotle it is a thing said in different ways. And these diverse ideas of existence proposed to us become all the more numerous, first, as our thought gives birth, so to speak, to the idea of truth, of nontemporal existence, of existence in a time that is no longer time but a sort of dead time; and then as this thought can be concentrated even on perceptions and judgments, which generates multiple existences and times—at least in appearance.

If, therefore, we are compelled to choose among these modes of existence, if, that is, existence is forced to choose existence, we could suggest that what exists above all, on the one hand, is that which resists our effort, and on the other hand, the effort of the subject in relation to that which resists. Existence would be defined by the resistance of the exterior to the interior, by the effort of the interior upon the exterior, and above all by the relation and union of the two. For there is also a union of feeling between this interior and exterior. We have chosen in this way simply because it is perhaps in the idea of resistance and in the idea of effort that the idea of existence is presented with intensity. We therefore link together the idea of existence with the idea of intensity.

This does not yet provide us with the structure of existence. Existence, to exist, signifies, etymologically, to exit from, *ex-sistere*, to exit either from the kingdom of the possible or from the absolute. What stands out from among the sum total of possibilities or separates itself from the absolute exists. However, this idea of detachment does not sufficiently characterize existence in itself. It is not only in relation to this totality, to this whole from which it detaches itself, but is it perhaps also in itself that existence is a detachment, an act of shattering itself? In this sense we are tempted to say that by itself existence is imperfection, that it appears as a rupture from the absolute, as, in itself, a wound, an estrangement.

Yet immediately we must contradict this idea: simultaneous with this imperfection and wounding, existence is also, and constantly, a manner of achievement and perfection. This is a classical idea; it can be found in Aristotle, with the notion of entelechy, and in Descartes, for whom the degrees of existence correspond to the degrees of perfection. More recently, and in a concrete form, we encounter it again in Whitehead.

Thus just as we have seen that existence is simultaneously the existence of the subject who expends effort, and of the object that resists him, an existence of a subject that is opposed and united to the object, we also see existence as separating and splitting apart and also as being accomplished and united to itself.

We could also say that existence is decision. This leads us toward Jaspers. Existence is decision but this decision is determined by the given [la donnée] that I am. I am given to myself in a specific way, and this decision is often only a kind of illusion, or, at least, it is only a choice between possibilities retrospectively discovered.

Let us retain from this discussion that existence is both decision and given, choice and nonchoice. And let us conclude that existence will never be able to be described or circumscribed except by apparently contradictory concepts, choice and nonchoice. In this way we see that this existence is not susceptible to being deduced *starting from* something else, from that something that classical philosophy called *essence*. Just now we defined existence by means of intensity, now we define it by means of irreducibility. Even so, it is still true that we are describing a sense of existence rather than an idea of existence.

Existence, such as we have described it up to this point, is perhaps too narrow; we should add that there is existence only if there is content to it. If existence is reduced to existence it does not exist. It only exists by means of its content; the existence of an "I" only exists through the other or others. It is perhaps because of too great a detachment from the other or others—a detachment that at least characterizes certain dimensions of the contemporary world—that certain philosophers have thought that there could be consciousness of existence only in feelings like boredom, anguish or sin (Kierkegaard), or nausea (Sartre).[1] It does not seem necessary, however, to have recourse to these feelings in order to be conscious of existence, if it is true that existence is not only an existence of the "I" but also union with another. Hence existence has content, and which is rich. There is existence only where there is content and an object.[2]

The descriptions of the existentialists risk making existence into that which least exists, an abstraction. Concrete existence is always existence before a task, in an action or facing another being. An existence is a relation with something other than oneself.

We could place in opposition the thought of a philosopher like Bosanquet and that of a religious thinker like Kierkegaard. Clearly Kierkegaard does not completely negate the "other," but he often (not always) reduces existence to a meditation on a single, divine other. According to Kierkegaard, I take hold of my existence in meditation before God. The two positions are antithetical: on the one hand, there is Kierkegaard and especially anyone who would push thought further by detaching the human being not only from every human other, but even from God; on the other hand, there is the position of Bosanquet, who attempts to expand continually the content of existence. These two positions each have their particular danger: one, an intensity that

1. This very idea of nausea as source of consciousness of existence was glimpsed by a disciple of Heidegger, Levinas, who has today, however, distanced himself from his master.

2. The philosophy of existence is a philosophy of transcendence. Existence is ecstasy, in the primitive sense of the word, an exit outside of the self; the human being is such inasmuch as it is standing outside of itself, in order to be in proximity to what is manifested. In this way the phenomenon of intentionality is most deeply understood. *Dasein* itself is outside of itself, is projected beyond. Existence transcends. The two ideas of existence and transcendence are reconnected in the idea of being-in-the-world, in the idea of being-with.

is too great; the other, a richness that is too great. If it is true that the painter and the sculptor are absorbed in the work they undertake, then it is also true for the philosopher, who, like Bosanquet, orients his effort toward a maximum enrichment, of doing something so that he no longer exists in the sense of the term "to exist"; his overly opulent opulence may lead to the nullification of his ego, an I that becomes the sum total of all the works that he admires as aesthetician or philosopher. On the other side, the inverse position equally runs the risk of dissolving the I in an overly intense intensity that is purely subjective. We should also emphasize the eminent value of poverty, of a spirit that withdraws into the unicity of a passion or a thought. The mystics above all have insisted on this idea.

Let me briefly clarify the idea of the feeling of existence. We could wonder about the relation between existence and the I. This is a problem that is capable of being clarified by means of, for example, the work of Proust. Proust observes his I undergoing a process of separation. He insists on what he calls the irregularities of the heart; there is no longer anything but phenomena without substance. This is an original appearance. We could set opposite this idea one exposed by Ramon Fernandez in his book *De la personnalité*, namely that there is truly existence only if there is a recovery of these phenomena in a permanent I, if there is at least the appearance of a certain center, by relation to which these phenomena become ordered. There must be a core and even—if these metaphors are compatible—a sort of radiation [extending out from it].

But here we find a new antinomy of existence. Existence is surely this re-entry into the self or this return to the self, but it is also (Bosanquet), an exit from the self. There is not even necessarily a link between the feeling of existence and the feeling of the "I" who exists. There can be existence and the disappearance of the "I," and not only in the moments of collapse described by Sartre in *Nausea*, but also in instants of intense plenitude. Being rendered anonymous, delivered from his or her "I," is the goal of mysticisms. It is also what André Gide has proposed on occasion. This would be the existence of an I who would no longer be me, who would be, so to speak, outside of me. These two moments of "outside me" and "for me" move us closer to a dialectic rather like

Hegel's. Hegel saw well the I as union of these two moments, of the opposition of something to me and of the withdrawing into the self.[3]

This analysis shows us that we find ourselves less before an existence than before a feeling of existence. This will cause us to pass from the phenomenology of existence to the study of existence as something that we absolutely cannot reach. We could also be led there through the intervention of Aristotle, when he highlights the fact that being is something different for each kind of being, or by Berkeley, when he critiques the idea of existence in general.

It will then be said that existence does not let itself be defined, since there is the existence of the "I," of the "you," of "him or her," of "that." This very conjugation of the verb *to exist*, its repercussions in thought, proves that no means exists by which we can characterize existence in a single manner. The diverse existences that we have enumerated are in no way identical. Even if we restrain ourselves to the [bare] existence of the "I," we still repeat the conjugation: "I have existed" and "I will exist" are not identical to "I exist." It could even be said that existence arises rather from "I will exist" or "I existed," than from "I exist" in the sense that everything I understand about myself is from either the past or future, and above all from the future if we are to believe Kierkegaard and Heidegger: according to them, it is starting from the future that I ceaselessly construct *myself*. Existence will then tend to be defined by regret or hope. This forces me to consider that I am able to speak about existence only from outside of it, from behind it or before it, without ever managing to remain interior to it. I am forced to remain at a certain distance from my existence. This is the human condition. It has been said that human existence is essentially a questioning of existence. In reality, the questioned falls silent or disguises itself when it questions itself. I therefore do not think that human existence can

3. It would be necessary to study also—and this is essential—the relations of existence and time. It would have to be determined in what sense existence happens in space and time, such that we conceive them on the surface, then in this concrete time that Bergson calls *duration*, in the tragic time that Heidegger attempts to define, and how finally at certain moments existence seems to attain a supratemporal level.

consist in questioning itself. On the contrary, the questioning runs the risk of making its existence vanish.[4] Existence flees before itself.

We thus return to an idea analogous to that of Jaspers, the idea of the failure of every interrogation of existence, and even the idea of failure in general.

However, I do not think that existence is uniquely in the past or future. It is in act—or in acts—that the existing being is destroyed and built up, for existence, of itself, is ceaseless destruction and construction. And it is in the acts by which this existent not only witnesses itself in the past or future, but is constituted in the very present as being the one who has this or that future or this or that past. This is what the Kierke-gaardian idea of repetition signifies.[5] The I, the individual as me, is the one who puts his or her seal on something from the past and says, "I am doing something that genuinely constitutes me." The same idea recurs as an element in the Nietzschean conception of the eternal return, the idea that at every instant the existing being intervenes in his or her existence through his or her "yes" or "no"—that one can or wants to assert oneself.

The problem of existence is not resolved theoretically, but practically, by the feeling that one has of being capable, to a certain degree, of reconciling one's past, future, and present.

Actually, every response to the question of existence is unsatisfying; the question is too general. The lone word, *existence*, is too vague for the feeling of existence that we had to describe. When someone says, "I exist," a boundary exists between "I" and "exist" just as another, insurmountable boundary persists between the felt "I" and the expressed "I." Furthermore, when we attempt to look at it, the feeling of existence flees our gaze.

It only lives powerfully when it is hidden.

---

4. A study could be attempted on the categories of existence such as boredom, work, leisure, risk, and even hope, regret, defeat, resignation, fate.

5. There is also a notion of repetition in Proust: he is felt to exist when he joins—or rather when there is joined in him—a past instant and a present instant. But in Kierkegaard the will, the intensity of the will, has more room, as it were, and the existence that one reaches is not an existence in a manifestation of eternity but an existence in time.

On the Idea of Transcendence

BAD TRANSCENDENCIES

If we want to speak of transcendence, perhaps we should be on guard against false transcendencies. Hegel denounced Romantic transcendence: a *Jenseits* [afterworld] conceived as a horizon that recedes without ceasing, but which in truth is not; Nietzsche denounced classical transcendence: a higher world conceived as justification for a morality of which one could trace a wholly immanent genealogy. And James denounced the transcendence of certain philosophies derived from Platonism.

IMMANENT REASONS FOR THE ATTRACTION OF TRANSCENDENCE

Without a doubt, one of the reasons that the idea of transcendence is so attractive is that when we think it, we think that we are thinking both a movement and its end [*terme*], which negates this movement. We do not only think the movement but its end; we do not only think the end, but the movement. To the idea of effort we join the idea of end by which this effort, in being accomplished, is annihilated. We are thinking something as unthinkable. Within ourselves we awaken—following the terminology of Jaspers—a thought that is not, properly speaking, thinkable.

As Kierkegaard sensed, it is by contact with something that negates it that a human being becomes most intensely conscious of its existence. He also had the feeling that this harsh relation within which we find ourselves, this enslavement to a superior principle, is a means of escaping a kind of powerless liberalism that he felt to be a prison.

At the same time, when we speak of transcendence we have the sentiment of a secret in which we participate.

Transcendence is at once a no and a yes. It is a yes that is posed to all of our affirmations; it is a no that is the affirmation of something beyond all of our affirmations.

ALTERITY, NEGATIVITY, TRANSCENDENCE

The man who thinks, like the man who lives, is placed within a context. The past, the object, and the *you* are implied by every thought, even the thought that negates them, just as food is necessary for the being that swallows it.

This is alterity, it is not yet transcendence.

Thought is able to become aware that there is a negativity of negativity, other than this negativity of negativity that it constitutes through its own development. It conceives transcendence when it sees this limit imposed on its activity.

TRANSCENDENCE AND MOVEMENT OF TRANSCENDENCE

If transcendence-as-movement is explained by transcendence-as-end, then, properly speaking, there is no longer transcendence.

The same thing applies when transcendence-as-end is explained by transcendence-as-movement.

Thus there is a tension between movement and its end. Neither the end nor the movement should be considered as given, either one by the other, or one without the other.

TRANSCENDENCE, CONSCIOUSNESS, AND UNCONSCIOUSNESS

It is thus necessary to say that if there is transcendence, then there is consciousness of transcendence. This consciousness of transcendence is tied to the feeling and idea of distance, consciousness implying distance in relation to that of which one is conscious.

On the other hand, if transcendence is attained, consciousness disappears; it can only be attained in the unconsciousness of oneself and of transcendence.

RELATIONS OF IMMANENCE AND TRANSCENDENCE

We no longer see immanence when we are in transcendence. In a sense, a symphony is reducible to vibrations, but this truth is not worth much for the one who understands and admires the symphony. The symphony has a meaning that transcends the truth of mathematical propositions, which can explain it from a certain point of view. Similarly, when one attains the highest point of the movement of transcendence, there is no longer any separation between immanence and transcendence.

Yet there is no means of thinking immanence without transcendence, no more than the opposite. It is necessary to conceive them as the one piercing through the other and the other re-encompassing it.

We can only think transcendence through thinking that in a certain manner we are immanent to it (we could call this "immersion" [*immergence*]), and we can only think immanence through thinking that in a certain manner we are transcendent to it.

Immersion [*immergence*] is the immanence of immanence in transcendence.

As defined by Alexander, emersion [émergence] is the transcendence of immanence by relation to immanence.

Therefore between transcendence and immanence there is a collection of relations that appear to be contradictory. There is a struggle between transcendence and immanence—if it is true that we find ourselves not before a transcendence that merely rebukes us, but before a transcendence that shatters the very élan that it has provoked.

TRANSASCENDENCE AND TRANSDESCENDENCE

A hierarchy or even hierarchies of transcendence can be conceived. If we can put it this way, there is a hierarchy directed toward the below, of which, say, Lawrence had been aware when he presented the unknown God beneath us, in the depths of being. There is not only a transascendence, but also a transdescendence.

TRANSCENDENCE TOWARD IMMANENCE

There is a movement of transcendence directed toward immanence. Here transcendence transcends itself.

Perhaps this is the greatest transcendence: to transcend transcendence, to fall back into immanence.

There would therefore be a second immanence after transcendence destroys itself.

We could conceive the idea of transcendence as necessary in order to destroy belief in a thought that only knows itself and in order then to make us feel our immersion in an immanence other than thought.

But if this destructive idea ought to be destroyed in turn, it is never completely destroyed, it is never completely transcended, and it remains in the background of the mind, like the idea of a lost paradise whose hoped for, lamented, and lost presence founds the value of our attachment to the here below.

Subjectivity and Transcendence

I.

A. Subjectivity and transcendence are two ideas that, from the philosophical point of view, characterize the thought of Kierkegaard. Or rather, it is the junction of the two that characterizes his thought. The tension inherent to subjectivity is explained by the presence of transcendence. By becoming more subjective, by closing in on itself, the subject suddenly discovers the transcendent. The soul alone before God alone: here we return to the ideas of Plotinus. But the soul is much more closed in on itself, and God enclosed in God, than in Plotinus and the mystics who followed the Neoplatonists. There is not in Kierkegaard this confluence of souls into God, and this expansion, this overflowing of God in souls. Rather, there is a much more powerful force of negation, an all-the-more irreducible opposition of individualities. And this is one of the causes of Kierkegaardian anguish.

A second cause of this anguish is the presence of evil. A being is in anguish because it does not know what it is facing, whether it

[The text of this chapter was originally presented to the Société française de philosophie on the evening of Dec. 4, 1937. It is reproduced here with very little change. The first part of this text (I. A–B and II. A–B) was distributed to the participants in advance of the meeting. It was then followed by an oral presentation by Wahl (the text of which follows) and then an extended discussion.]

stands before a beneficent transcendence or a maleficent transcendence, whether it faces God or a demonic power; it does not know if the movement that it accomplishes is a movement of "transascendence" or "transdescendence."

B. In Kierkegaard, these ideas are enveloped in an atmosphere of theology and morality. We could ask if *transascendence* is necessarily good and *transdescendence* is necessarily evil. On this point, the teachings of Blake, of Gide in his *Dostoyevsky*, of Lawrence, and of John Cowper Powys would be invaluable. For them it is a matter of returning to something elementary, savage: "angel or demon, it does not matter."

Additionally, we could ask if we need to retain the theological aspect of subjectivity and transcendence. Transcendence is not necessarily God or the devil. It could simply be nature, which is no less mysterious than the God of orthodoxies and the God of heterodoxies.

II.

A. Observing philosophical developments in Germany, we can see that those most inspired by Kierkegaard, Heidegger and Jaspers, developed his philosophy through the ideas of "being-in-the-world," "communication," and "historicity" (these last two, first presented in the thought of Kierkegaard, are highlighted by Jaspers).

At the same time, these two thinkers want to remain within the world that is ours; they refuse to follow Kierkegaard when he searches for "repetition" in a beyond, after having tried in vain to find it in this world.

B. Are they, however, completely delivered from the theological elements of Kierkegaardian thought? Both have tried to secularize the idea of sin, such as they found it in Kierkegaard and theology: Heidegger, in making sin the fall into the realm of the anonymous crowd, into the "They"; Jaspers, in an apparently more profound way, through identifying it with limitation. But this latter conception implies the idea that the good would be the totality, which Jaspers's thought does not seem capable of admitting.

In both thinkers one finds the idea of "repetition." But is this not, just like the theories of the instant or of the eternal return, an *Ersatz* of the idea of eternity?

Could a philosophy similar to that of Heidegger and Jaspers be conceived, and of which the attraction would not be partly explained by its inclusion of nostalgia for and an echo of the religious?

And if such a philosophy is conceivable, would it not risk dissolving into a general theory of existence, where all particularity, all historicity, all existence is excluded?

Perhaps that is where the problem faced by "existential philosophy" lies, and which is exposed to a double danger: either of being joined to theology too directly, or of detaching too completely from every concretely given.

This is what can lead us to ask ourselves if some existences like those of Rimbaud or Van Gogh or Nietzsche (or Kierkegaard) are not actually more "existential" and more truly philosophical than the philosophies of existence. But these latter at least have the merit of making us more acutely sense the value of the former.

Kierkegaard places us before the *here* and *now*, whereas, on the contrary, for Hegel, the here and now ought to be reabsorbed by a dialectic into generalities, into universalities that are more and more immense.[1] This here and this now is evidently not uniquely the bodily here and now. They both open onto a subjectivity, and it is before subjectivity that Kierkegaard places us. But this subjectivity itself, for him, takes its value, its reality, from the fact that it is found in the presence of *another*, of the absolute *other*, of the absolutely different, the transcendent.

Subjectivity should not try, as it does in thinking like Hegel's, to assimilate this other or even be assimilated to it. No. It is found in

1. [The following is the text Wahl presented *viva voce* to the meeting of 1937. There he introduced these remarks with the following words: "I would simply like to pose some questions in relation to Kierkegaard and contemporary philosophy. To introduce this subject one could begin by opposing Kierkegaard to Hegel. I will do so very briefly" ("Subjectivité et transcendance," *Bulletin de la Société française de philosophie* 37, no. 5 (1937): 166).]

the presence of this other in order to collide with it. And this collision is all the more violent as this other, in the thought of Kierkegaard, assumes an essentially paradoxical aspect. This other is in fact the eternal rendered temporal. And it is this that Kierkegaard calls the absolute protestation against immanence, the fact that the eternal became historical.

It is at this moment that we must break with thought, at the moment when we feel that our eternal beatitude depends on our relation with something historical, and that this something historical is nothing other than the eternal.

This relation must be lived. We must live it isolated in our thought, somehow both tightly coiled up within our present and reaching out for our future.

Evidently, we cannot define this other. But at least we are able to say that we are aware of it through the relation that we have with it. And here a new paradox emerges. This *other* is fundamentally the *one* of the first hypothesis of the *Parmenides*, which is absolutely without relation with anything; and yet this one without relation only exists through the relation in which we find ourselves with it.

This is in fact the most internal relation, the relation, for Kierkegaard, with something from the outside; the absolute transcendent is only revealed through this absolutely immanent relation with the individual.

If we are concerned, indeed, with another than ourselves, this other can only be the absolute other, so that the intensity of our passion signifies that we are in relation with something which can only be the eternal and absolute. The intensity of this relation is such that by the very fact that we enter into it, it gives us this other element [*terme*]—this other limit [*terme*] which in a sense can never be given. And it is in this way that what is subjective to the highest degree must be considered as relating to what is objective to the highest degree.

But, in spite of the abstract terms in which Kierkegaard presents it, and in which I have presented it after him, this is nothing other (as he says) than a description of belief. Belief is necessarily belief in another. This other, in whose existence we are infinitely interested, can only be God. And this movement, this relation that I am describing, which is both exit toward the other and passionate interiority, is still nothing other than the paradox of belief. We could say then that Kierkegaard entered into the domain of paradox and contradiction in order simply to give a faithful description of the phenomenon of belief.

Once the individual is found in this relation, somehow, by the force of this paradoxical passion within him and which is belief, he will work toward the annihilation of his thought. Here the phenomenon of anguish is produced, because of the co-presence of this subjective thinker and this transcendent object. We see at the same time how Kierkegaard's conception radically differs, at least most of the time, from mysticism: there is, generally speaking, no fusion with the other. Though Kierkegaard lived certain moments of ecstasy or near-ecstasy, ordinarily the other is a sort of resistant being who is before him and from which he is separated.

Kierkegaardian anguish has a second cause, the presence of evil. This second cause is very profoundly bound up with the first. From the moment that this other than me is distant from me, I will not communicate directly with it and I will have the incessant sense that I may be mistaken about its essence. From here the idea emerges that we are never sure of being in the presence of God. And this element of uncertainty subsists in belief as Kierkegaard defines it. This is a new element which brings his description of belief to completion.

This anguish becomes even greater as we have the idea that God might be tempting us, and at the same time the fear that we might be tempting God in some way, an idea which appears quite often in Kierkegaard. From here emerge certain characteristics of his thought, when he finds himself in the presence of moral problems: on the one hand, either the suspension of the ethical, as in *Fear and Trembling*, where he shows how Abraham ought to leave behind the rules of morality in order to obey God; or even, on the other hand, the idea that it is necessary to sink into the depths of sin in order to have access to faith, or finally, on the contrary, the conception of religious ethics.

One could without a doubt interpret in a different way the hesitation which is produced in the individual faced with that which exceeds him. The individual can be surpassed in two different directions: he can be surpassed from below as from above, either by mysterious forces that meet back up with the animal dimensions of being (and which are perhaps not bad simply for that), or, secondly, by forces of nature recognized as superior.

And, at the same time, I wonder why there is in Kierkegaard this will to paradox and contradiction. Why? The intensification of the existence of the individual. But Kierkegaard himself knows that the existence of the individual is a paradox in itself. It is not simply God who is paradox in coming to earth, but we ourselves are paradoxes by being, as Kierkegaard put it, a union and contradiction of the finite and infinite.

To have the sense of paradox, is it so necessary to refer to those same beliefs to which Kierkegaard refers? Is not the vision of what surrounds us full of realities that are extremely paradoxical, like knowledge, the person, or even things?

———

One could say that Heidegger and Jaspers are in a sufficiently similar relation to Kierkegaard and Husserl, and in a contradictory relation to both on certain points.[2] Husserl separates essences from existences, and Kierkegaard separates the individual and the world, whereas for Heidegger, existence is essence, and this existence is being and being in the world.

Taking account of all the nuances—even more, the profound differences—that should be established between these two philosophers, what Heidegger and Jaspers have somehow added to the thought of Kierkegaard are the ideas of "being in the world," of communication, and of "*Geschichtlichkeit*," historicity. The individual is bound to the world in a fundamental manner. And Heidegger always insists, and in a very beautiful way, on his radical isolation.

The difficulty of speaking of transcendence in Heidegger seems to be because this word has different senses in his thought. First he speaks of the transcendence of being in relation to nothing. Then he

———

2. [The text of Wahl's remarks from 1937 continues here. This section is introduced in the original text with the following words: "From Kierkegaard I pass in summary to Heidegger and Jaspers" (168).]

employs the word *transcendence* when he characterizes our relation with *being-in-the-world*. And in the third place he employs the word *transcendence* when he describes our life in its way of being always out in front of itself, projecting toward the future. So existence is transcendent starting from nothing, it is transcendent in relation to the world, or the world is transcendent in relation to it, and it is transcendent in relation to itself.

But all of this only makes us more acutely feel what characterizes existence for Heidegger, namely, finitude. The two ideas of transcendence and finitude are tied for Heidegger; and what he places in the foreground is the idea of the abandonment of being, a sort of essential poverty of being. His is not a philosophy of abundance, *poros*, but on the contrary, one could say, a philosophy of *peneia*, of essential misery.

I said that in Heidegger "transcendence" has multiple applications; in Jaspers the idea is by definition very difficult to elucidate. Jaspers, by starting from the fact that in myself there are a lot of things which do not depend on me, arrives at the idea that I am in some way given to myself, and thus there are some things which exceed me. The transcendent will also be that which, by opposition to myself, I conceive as essentially one, unconditioned, independent, and as a reality in which possibility cannot be distinguished from reality.

In Heidegger and Jaspers one also finds this same junction between the ideas of subjectivity and transcendence that I have noted in Kierkegaard. For example, in Heidegger, it is above all in transcending toward the world that a subjectivity is realized, or even that transcendence can only be revealed by the ontological interpretation of subjectivity; it is in returning to itself that the individual discovers the other than itself.

We can bring in from here the analyses that Heidegger makes of certain feelings that put us in the presence of the world in its totality, not only the feeling of angst on which he particularly insists, but also, as he took care to say, feelings like boredom or joy. These feelings that bind us to what is most personal within us cause to rise up before our mind a whole—even more than a whole, the totality of the world—at least sometimes, in certain particular joys, in certain anguishes, certain particular moments of boredom; through the personality we come to vast impersonal feelings.

In Jaspers this same connection can be found. For example, in such phrases as these: "The more profoundly I press into myself, the more I feel solidarity with the one who is a stranger to me." And again: "Transcendence is revealed in my attitude toward it. It is the existence that I can only attain by my more profound subjectivity."

And both Heidegger and Jaspers, after having thus highlighted this idea of transcendence, enact a movement rather analogous to the movement that Kierkegaard accomplished in returning toward imma-nence, with the help of the idea that they borrow, it seems to me, from Kierkegaard: "repetition."

Repetition is the act in which the past is taken up again, some-how, outside of the past, and newly made present, reaffirmed. One could compare it to the way in which Aristotle defined substance: *to ti han einai.* The individual should be that which it was. It is the act of "remaining what one was" and of thus being reaffirmed.

Along with Kierkegaard, and perhaps more than he, they give this idea of repetition a metaphysical allure, analogous to what Nietzsche gave to the eternal return. By repetition we fashion a unity out of the present, past, and future. We attain a moment where there is an absolute marriage of what Heidegger calls "the three ecstasies of time."

Regarding these philosophies, we could wonder—it is the first question I asked myself—if some elements of beliefs do not remain in them from which they wanted to be distinguished and by which they are in fact distinguished. The strongest feeling that exists in Heidegger and which colors all of his work is the sense that man is thrown into the world, "*entworfen,*" and abandoned, the idea of the "*Entworfenheit*" of man, of finitude, of a deserted finitude, one could almost say an accursed finitude.

Is there not something here that is only explained by the memory, by remembering other ideas, and not explained through itself but by relation with that from which Heidegger has broken?

In the second place, it seems to me that the idea of repetition, in its metaphysically extreme form, could call forth criticisms, some objec-tions, when it takes the form of absolute repetition, when it wants to be the absolute unification of moments of time. What is it that the philosopher wants to accomplish? He wants to find a *nunc stans* in our temporality, and the task is certainly arduous.

As for transcendence such as they define it, it seems to me that here again some questions come to mind since we have seen the multiplicity of meanings that it has in Heidegger. And in Jaspers, it is definitely difficult to grasp, which is doubtlessly natural, since by definition transcendence cannot be completely grasped, but this is aggravated when he says that I am only able to grasp it by unifying myself, and, at the same time, that he wants, however, to preserve it as transcendence and as other—and this, so that, on the one hand, transcendence ought to be me in my extreme unity and, on the other hand, something both different from me and opposed to me.

But one of the gravest criticisms, I believe, that one could make of Jaspers's theory is that he tells us that all philosophy consists of a choice, of a radical option, but he himself is content to establish the theory that all philosophy consists in a radical option, that is to say, that he does not decide—and this, so that if we were to delve deeper into this thought, we would come to affirm that existence such as it is here defined is in a sense the least existential of all since it is able, as it were, to see very well; it stands back and justifies every choice, but in itself it only justifies the decision of others and does not choose for itself.

Here the importance of Jaspers's work is not diminished, but it is no longer necessary perhaps to pigeonhole his philosophy within the same framework as others: it is a general theory of philosophies, a work of an observer of philosophies; it is not the act of a philosopher choosing for himself his symbol, his figure. If it is such an act, it loses its general value and is no longer a theory of philosophies in general.

At the root of these philosophies of Heidegger and Jaspers is a double feeling of regret and hope, which corresponds to the two ecstasies of time—to speak like Heidegger—the past and the future and which, as it were, intones the rhythm of time; it is the double feeling of paradise lost and of this paradise regained: repetition.

In thinking through the efforts of these philosophers I have come to think that perhaps one could find in others outside of philosophy similar attempts that draw closer to existence. And the names that have by chance come to mind—by chance indeed, but selecting from among those that I most admire—are Rimbaud, Van Gogh, and Nietzsche. Yet all three possess in a very strong manner precisely these two attitudes of subjectivity and transcendence. That which captivates us in a work of Van Gogh is precisely the intensity of his feeling and the fact that— to take back up the phrase of Cézanne—he "created the image" [*faisait l'image*]. And concerning Nietzsche's thought, there is, on the one hand, the Overman and, on the other hand, the Eternal Return, which symbolize what is most absurd, the immanent symbolizing the pure transcendent by relation to our thought.

Even so, my personal preference of Rimbaud or Van Gogh or Nietzsche over Heidegger and Jaspers does not seem to me to disagree with the main current of their thought. For Heidegger says very well that the metaphysics of human reality is not only a metaphysics about [*sur*] reality, it is metaphysics coming necessarily to occur as reality. Perhaps this is what we find in Rimbaud or Nietzsche. And when Heidegger, in one of his most recent works, speaks of Hölderlin, it is perhaps not first a very different sentiment that animates him: the idea that art is also grasped by the individual as a relation with the transcendent. And for a stronger reason, one could say, Jaspers could be in agreement with what I am saying here, because he possesses very strongly this sense of the value of art; moreover he also refers to Van Gogh, and it is above all in the individual as existence that he finds the reality of philosophy.[3]

3. [This brings to a close Wahl's integral remarks from 1937.]

On the Idea of Being

For Parmenides being is a plenitude, a density to be more precise. But this determined density becomes, with Melissus, indeterminate, and in the first hypothesis of Plato's *Parmenides*, it becomes an emptiness.

Concerning the idea of being, the roles of Plato and Aristotle seem to have been twofold. First, we can find in them elements of a critique of the idea of being. According to Plato, being is on the same footing as nonbeing and is no easier to know than it; being is not the aggregate of beings but an idea that is other in relation to certain other ideas; it is one idea in relation to others. And Aristotle shows that the idea of being is not unique, no more than is the very idea of unity; one should not search for a unique being, but for each genre of being, that which is being and one; the idea of being will be the analogy of relations between each of these beings and the being of each.[1] But second, Plato

---

1. Heidegger demonstrates how the analogy of being ought to be pushed even further than it has been by the Aristotelians and the Thomists. The being of human being is not instrumental being, nor the being of a truly subsistent, nor extended being. Here there are many kinds of different beings (Lecture Course of 1928–29 [*Einleitung in die Philosophie*, GA 27], lecture 8).

It is very characteristic of Heidegger that all the analogies of being (being of the human being, being of the instrument, being of the extended thing, being of truths) and all the ambiguities of being (being as essence, as existence, as relation,

shows that this being is something irreducible by the very fact that it is a third term in relation to each of the terms in relation. It should also be noted that he speaks of a being that is being at its perfection. For his part, Aristotle, by means of his affirmation of something that is fundamentally being, by his theory of substance, prepares the way for the Neoplatonic conception of a hierarchy of beings and then the Scholastic conception.[2]

Descartes, following medieval philosophers who accepted a kind of equivalence of transcendentals, only brings to a completion the Scholastic conception when he identifies being and value, and builds a hierarchy of beings that is a hierarchy of values.

With Kant, we find a reversal of these different theories of being: being is not a relation, as the Platonic and Aristotelian critiques of the idea of being tried to pretend; it is not a quality and a value, as the constructive parts of these philosophies tried to pretend, followed by the Scholastics and Descartes. It is neither copula nor predication. It is position.

But, Hegel will add, repeating an idea found in Plato, this position emerges only through negation. Being is negativity at the same time as it is position.

But, Bergson will add in turn, negativity is second; or, in any case, negation is second; affirmation is first.

---

as affirmation of truth) are left in the shadows, left in the background, in the "is" of judgment, which is like a middle, indifferent "is."

2. To take up again an example from recent philosophy, for Heidegger every perception implies an idea about the being of the perceived, or at least a sentiment, a presentiment, of the being of the perceived, as every usage of an instrument implies an idea, a sentiment, or more precisely a presentiment of the instrument.

But from here there ensue some difficulties within Heidegger's philosophy. Does he not take as concrete what in truth is abstract? And how does one make out of these different ideas of being a single idea? And if it is true that there is only being if there is *Dasein*, can being be studied independently of *Dasein*? It could doubtlessly be admitted that, all the while affirming that the comprehension of being is a property of *Dasein*, being is independent of this comprehension. Heidegger has not sufficiently demonstrated this; he has surely reserved this for later work.

Whatever the case, like Plato and Aristotle, after critiquing the idea of a unity of being, Heidegger reestablishes this idea.

And this affirmation is an affirmation of a plenitude.

Now we find ourselves face to face with the affirmation of Parmenides, but this time pronounced in the face of a Heraclitean world.

BEING AND JUDGMENT

Plato and Aristotle have shown that it is necessary to distinguish between *to be* and *to be true*. This was all the more necessary since the verb "to be," in Greek, meant both *it is* and *it is true*. But it is also appropriate to observe that the identity of these two meanings is well founded: to affirm that a thing is, is to affirm that the judgment that affirms it is true. The idea of being implies the existence of a being that affirms being. The idea of being, like every idea, only has a place in the world of judgments, the universe of discourse.

ANTINOMIES OF THE IDEA OF BEING

But it should also be said that, like every idea, the idea of being is the affirmation of something other than that which does the act of affirming, and has position through our thought of something that is outside of our thought, and is the position of something outside of position.

This something resists us and at the same time fulfills our desires; for Maine de Biran and Scheler, being is that which resists; for Marcel, along with Biran and Scheler, it is what fulfills our expectation.

Being is what happens [*se produit*] and what is permanent; and in order to grasp it the mind will always hesitate between the idea of a substance and the idea of an event.

Being is seen by its action, but there is a center, other than this action, from where it radiates.

Being is relative independence; but it is dependence at the same time; it is existence, which means that it detaches from an obscure depth, and it is knowledge—if we take this word in the sense that Claudel gives to it, as a participation or communion. In a first moment, being is closed in on itself as a here and now, and it is this that I have termed existence. But in a second moment it is participation in every-thing else, in relation to the other, to that which it is not, and which, however, it is. And it is this that I have termed knowledge.

Yet it would still have to be said that these antinomies themselves presuppose a rather artificial posing of the problem, as if we ourselves and being were opposite one another, whereas we are embedded in being and being is embedded within us. Between the thought of being and being there is a subterranean communication. The thought of being is being as well.

Fusion of the separated, separation of what is united—by this path one turns back toward the essence of Hegelianism.

We find this double function in judgment. The word being sepa-rates and at the same time unites.

It will thus tend to incline along one or the other of these slopes: thought will move toward analysis and will identify comprehension and dissection, or, moving toward synthesis, it will only be satisfied if it believes itself to be at the heart of the absolute.

BEING AND THE IDEA OF BEING

Nowhere do we see more clearly than in the idea of being what could be called the simultaneous marriage and divorce of language and reality. The most abstract and emptiest idea, the fullest feeling: one implies the other. (We could say the same thing about the ideas of *here* and *now*.)[3] This happens in such a way that after having said that the idea of being is being, it would be possible to say that being is not; I want to say that there is such an abundance of being in being that it cannot be designated by the little word *is*.

---

3. In his critique of the idea of being, as of the here and now, Hegel believed himself to be able to come to a conclusion about the indeterminateness of the feelings that these words express from the fact that the words are indeterminate. As Koyré has so well remarked, for Hegel language incarnates spirit, and the life of language is the life of spirit (see "Hegel à Iena," *Revue philosophique* [1934]: 283).

On the Absolute

THE DIVISIONS OF THE ABSOLUTE

Being is, nonbeing is not. This affirmation leads Parmenides to posit the absolute. But was this a uniquely logical and ontological enunciation or the expression of a mystical vision at the same time?

This question of historical order leads us to pose a more general question: will we reach the absolute by knowledge, will we reach it by feeling?

(Absolute movement, says Bergson, is felt movement.)

In the *Parmenides* Plato critiques the Eleatic philosopher, showing that if the One is purely one, we reach a transcendent absolute about which we can say nothing, and if the One is, we reach an immanent absolute about which we can say everything.

Therefore we see that the thought of the Absolute is refracted in the intellect and in feeling, and in its turn, the intelligence is refracted in a transcendent absolute and immanent absolute.

Perhaps we could even demonstrate an analogous refraction in feeling. Novalis's Romanticism and Romanticism in general conceives of feeling as fusion, as identification. A different conception, where beings remain separate in love—present, but present opposite one another, rather than present in one another—appeared with Scheler, with Lawrence, and in France with Gabriel Marcel. These writers found in love the principle of alterity and transcendence.

We could say that the thought of the absolute is divided by entering into contact with our thought, and remains always beyond it.[1]

There is an absolute into which one sinks, and an absolute into which one collides.

There is an absolute that assimilates and an absolute that remains separated: one is that of Bradley, for example, the other is that of negative theology.

(Bradley's absolute is also Hegel's, but without the movement being too apparent that in Hegel causes inferior manifestations to pass into superior manifestations of the absolute. There comes about from here the similar rupture in Bradley between reality and appearance.)

They seem completely opposed, and yet the first leads to the second. Hence this would be the affirmation of the absolute: the affirmation that what is separated from all (ab-solutus) is at the same time what contains all (absolute in the ordinary sense).

(Transferring this affirmation to the practical domain, we arrive at the idea that in being detached from all, one is united to all.)

This divided absolute about which we are speaking is at the same time an absolutely united absolute.

THE BEYOND AND THE BELOW

We have said that the absolute *remains beyond.*

But if the absolute escapes language and thought, it is less so because its idea is the idea of something that is beyond, than because it is that of a below.

In the transcendent, there is simultaneously the transascendent and the transdescendent. But there is also the idea that these distinctions are futile.

---

1. Proclus spoke of the tearing apart of indivisible knowledge.

THE ABSOLUTE AND SPACE

Nowhere more so than when the subject is the absolute is it felt that our ideas are infested with spatial thinking. The very negation of space is still expressed and thought of in terms of space.

THE ABSOLUTE AND TIME

The absolute is represented as rest, and yet the thought of it is inseparable from the thought of a movement. This last affirmation leads to the affirmation of the necessity of a dialectic: Platonic dialectic, Hegelian dialectic.

As Plato says in the *Philebus,* there is, moreover in a different sense, a *genesis eis ousian.*

And the *Sophist* already gave rise to the thought that there is life and movement in being.

Enjoyment is likewise represented as rest, and one proceeds to enjoyment only through a movement.

The absolute separates, and the thought of the eternal partakes of time.

Plato says that perfect being is rest and movement.

Perhaps Rimbaud wanted to express the same vision:

Elle est retrouvée
Quoi? L'éternité.
C'est la mer mêlée au soleil.

Found again.
What? Eternity.
The sea mixed up with the sun.[2]

2. [Rimbaud's poetry is remarkably difficult to establish, given multiple versions and the uncertainty of dating the composition. The text provided in the

Nietzsche's eternal return is a matter of a hopeless effort to place the absolute in the ephemeral, to the great terror of men and the great joy of the Overman.

Thanks to the eternal return, the poet is right to say:

Aimez ce que jamais l'on ne verra deux fois,

Love everything you will not twice see,[3]

and the other poet is equally right to say:

Qu'est-ce que tout cela qui n'est pas éternel ?

What is all this that is not eternal?[4]

For the eternal is precisely that which ordinary men never suppose to see twice.

Under another form, the same union of sentiments is seen in Novalis and Proust.

Oxford World Classics critical edition is dated May 1872. The last two lines vary from what is, as quoted by Wahl, a single line:

Elle est retrouvée.
Quoi?—L'Éternité.
C'est la mer allée
Avec le soleil.

Found again. What?
Eternity.
The sea gone
With the sun.

Arthur Rimbaud, "Eternity," *Collected Poems* (French/English *en face*), trans. Martin Sorrell (Oxford: Oxford University Press, 2001), 180/181.]

3. [Alfred de Vigny, "La maison du Berger (III)," *Les destinées*, ed. V. L. Saulnier (Paris: Minard, 1967).]

4. [This line is the fourth of the penultimate quatrain of Charles-Marie Leconte de Lisle, "L'illusion suprême," *Poèmes tragiques* (rpt.; Paris: Hachette, Bibliothèque nationale de France, 2012.)]

This idea of the infinitely recurring instant, of an instant in which the future and past are united, is also present in Kierkegaard. On this point as well, Heidegger and Jaspers spring from Nietzsche and Kierkegaard.

But as I said, all this effort is hopeless and this idea of an eternal instant is a myth.

THE ABSOLUTE TODAY

There are some writers today who imagine themselves very far from the idea of the absolute, but their thought is dominated by this idea. What they search for in despair is this purity that they can no longer find in hope. What they seek in chance is absolute detachment from everything, a radical beginning and entrance into a completely different context where they can be arrested by something that is absolutely transcendent in relation to themselves.

THE ABSOLUTE AND THE PARTIAL

In Hegelianism, the absolute is the totality of relations (a view that ends up being intellectualized by Hamelin and sensualized by Bradley).

But the protestations of a philosophy founded on the study of focused and passionate visions of the world will always be brought to bear on this idea. I think of Jaspers's meditations on Kierkegaard's philosophy: an intense experience is more absolute than the relational totality of experiences. The absolute ought not to be thought in comprehension more than in extension. This is still to remain in a quantitative domain. If I can put it this way, it ought to be thought in intensity.

––––––––––

Hegel tried to clarify the idea of the absolute with the help of the idea of the concrete universal. After him, Bradley and above all Bosanquet defined it as a *world*.

But a poet like Blake sometimes puts us in the presence of the *particular minute*,[5] a tiny fragment of the universe, and he teaches us to find the absolute here.

ABSOLUTE AND RELATION WITH THE ABSOLUTE

The absolute only exists within the relation that we have with it. Such was Kierkegaard's idea: if we think absolutely (in an infinite tension with ourselves) then we feel the absolute (I say "feel" because it is necessary to employ some word or other).

The absolute is in the tension between it and myself. If there were an absolute that was like a datum, there would not be between it and us this tension that is essential to it—a tension that attempts to think that which escapes it: me, the absolute.

To exist, and, even more so, to exist absolutely, is to be aware of this insurgent ground of consciousness.

The absolute is the tension, which grounds it within me, and this that resists it outside of me, and the passage to the outside by means of what is more internal within us. At the same time, it is the destruction of these distinctions.

RELATION OF THE CRITIQUE OF THE ABSOLUTE
WITH BELIEF IN IT

Our thought of the absolute would be that it is not necessary to seek the absolute in the totality nor in eternity, but in the partial and in the ephemeral felt with intensity.

Our thought of the absolute is above all a critique, the critique of classical conceptions of the absolute.

However, it leaves intact the aspiration that was the origin of these conceptions. It itself inhabits the tension between this critique and this

5. [This italicized phrase is in English in the original.]

aspiration that escapes critique, because it is below and above all critique, rejoining us with what Boehme calls the *Grund* and Lawrence calls *the dark God.*

The thought of the absolute is the thought of this atmosphere and domain where I realize myself by destroying myself.

On Space and Time

The idea of space. I would first like to articulate the paradox that is born as soon as one draws together the two notions of space and the idea. Space is this in which we are, this present density of which we are a part. But the very words let escape what they want to communicate. For it is not a matter of "part" or "in": as soon as the idea of space arises in my mind, there also arises the negation that scientific speculation reaches with Whitehead, the negation of what one commonly intends by space. This is what I would like to say first, as a beginning.

But this beginning already presupposes another beginning. Here my dialectic is regressive because it is negative. This space that I am negating is the space that Descartes and Kant set their eyes on, the space necessary for science, moreover, not the vibrant space of our organs, the palpitating space of clouds, the space dug out by the Venetian baroque, which plays everywhere starting from columns and wheels of light, but also the space of the juxtaposition of undifferentiated points, the space that is not thought of as interiorly withdrawn but as apart and beyond.

Nevertheless we note that these two philosophers do not agree about the idea of space. Whereas Descartes sees only absolutely transparent relations for pure intelligence, Kant senses something qualitative and heterogeneous. We are tempted to say then that Kant is much closer than the Cartesians to the idea of a qualitative space, as I presented it at first in the false beginning that led me back (perhaps) toward a truer beginning.

Between Descartes and Kant there is Leibniz, whose perspective surely deserves to be mentioned. He is less profound on this point than Kant. Further, then, from my own thought (I mean this in a way that is at once modest and immodest), he sees in space a collection of purely intellectual relations. Although, more profoundly, he sees in space an order of relations, in a manner that is less thing-like, less realist (less productive of abstractions). Space is not for him an empty milieu; it is something that comes after, which comes from reflection on some originally given qualities. He is wrong to expel qualities from space; he is right to see that space derives from qualities and is an order of qualities.

What remains within our grasp? Space as negation of space, of the space necessary to mathematics and for action—what remains is space as interiorly withdrawn (words here fall short), as entanglement, intermingling, and which is opposed to space as apart and beyond. What matters is seeing the presuppositions and consequences entailed by these two ideas of space.

Clearly the first assumes the second. Here we meet back up with the discussion between the partisans of immanence and the partisans of transcendence: immanence is the negation of transcendence. But it becomes clear a little later that transcendence assumes negated immanence.

This is not surprising. Our mind only advances through negation, we only write by means of crossing out, and we only adjudge through dilemmas in which we accept one of the terms.

And I am always rediscovering this old thought by which I meet the negative theologian, a negative theology without God, a negative ontology—to wit, that negations speak a plenitude of reality situated beyond every negation. Consciousness chooses, differentiates, and draws out inseparable aspects.

Here we find ourselves already arriving at the point. I have now already said everything. Can we find another means by which to go further or somewhere else in order to escape this operation of mind that is always the same that I for one would really like to diversify or avoid altogether? What is the genesis of space itself? Few philosophers have attempted to respond to this difficult question. To my mind it invokes two names: Plotinus and Boehme. In the modern era no one has taken on this problem with the audacity of the authentic successor of Plotinus, Bergson.

Space conceived as outside is born from a sort of need for separation that exists within being, a need for an essential diaspora which, already visible in the domain of the intelligible, is accentuated to the degree that one moves toward the sensible. (Recall Bergson's beautiful passage in the last pages of *Creative Evolution* where he compares space with a nullity that, while being nothing, yet multiplies numbers. Recall then the beautiful vision of union in the ancients between the idea of emptiness and the idea of multiplicity. There is an analogy here between Plato and his contemporary, Democritus.) One could likely, and without too much implausibility, attribute this idea to Boehme (interpreted only a little), for whom space is the child of the wrath of God.

What differences emerge between Plotinus and Boehme! The space of Plotinus, akin to Plato's, despite all, lies on the path that leads to Cartesian science, of which it is the origin. Whereas the space of Boehme, at least as I present it, is even more akin to Whitehead's anti-Cartesian science. Like a word that is scratched out, it is thickly criss-crossed with qualitative streaks that are deep, sulphurous, and aching.

It is certainly necessary to realize that in this second (very brief and very insufficient) part of my study, I remain in the region of myth. And myth should not be eliminated. This is one of the great lessons of philosophy, of its history, and of Plato especially. It is especially necessary because everything that is not designated as myth is still speech—is still, therefore, myth. *Fabula narrator.* This leads me to wonder about the relations between the idea of space and the idea of unhappy consciousness. At the origin of the idea of space do we not find the more general idea of separation and perhaps even of time, direction, and tendency toward? But we should be careful not to slide in this way into panpsychism or, worse still, into that spiritualism that makes the world the product of the "creative activity of mind." If there exists a philosophy to which my mind says a loud "no," that is it. Yet, on the other hand, I am deeply attracted to the magical idealism of Novalis, which is rather similar. Should we thus say that at the root of the idea of space there is the fact that I do not see actualized everything toward which I strain, and that therefore there is a *toward*? Is personal dissatisfaction at the origin of the idea of space?

I am inclined to say so, or rather, to say that this is its—very general—symptom. Judgment in general is a similar dissatisfaction. The rose is also outside of the rose. And this is what the word *is* partly signifies. Here we meet back up with Bradley's theory of judgment and perhaps at the same time the idea for which the affirmation of an intelligible space is the translation. Space is the affirmation of dualities and pluralities.

And here the great problem of the interiority and exteriority of relations arises before my mind, as the English philosophy of the nineteenth century formulated it. Suddenly I better see the reason why I would not reach a successful conclusion that I already saw from the beginning. Space as affirmation of the exteriority of relation is also the affirmation of the interiority of relations.

The idea of relation is inadequate. And space is necessary for me, but it is necessary for it to break apart. It is necessary (to follow Jaspers's expression) that my thinking run aground.

I can at least say that, without having spent too much effort, I have approached a view that intensely unites space and my existence: space is my immersion in things, and it is my emersion out of things. Space is my existence, as it is inherence in things; it is my existence as much as it is a distance in relation to things and to myself.

Ainsi sur des béquilles avance ma philosophie,
Comme la sagesse de Dieu;
Elle n'a pas tout le temps pour arriver,
Mais elle sait que là où elle s'assoira, elle sera aussi bien qu'ailleurs,
Voyant une route très longue devant elle et derrière elle.
Les yeux bandés,
Des cornes sur son front,
Et pleurant sur sa tombe au seuil de Chanaan.

And on crutches advances my philosophy,
Like the wisdom of God;
It does not have all time to arrive,
But it knows that where it will come to sit will be as good as
    anywhere,
Seeing a very long road ahead and behind.
Eyes covered,
Horns on its head,
And weeping over its tomb on the threshold of Canaan.

Pleurant sur sa tombe/Weeping over its tomb. I mean that this land beyond relations, this land of the finite center so well described by Bradley, is always destroyed as soon as I become aware of it. There is only unhappy consciousness. There is only consciousness that is set at a certain distance from itself. In this sense we could say that consciousness is space.

But in this same sense I would also say that consciousness, being the negation of space, can, in a specifically absent manner and as weeping [*pleurante*]—I almost said "[as a] whiner" [*pleurarde*]—accomplish its happiness.

It is appropriate, however, to pose a formidable question here. Science has succeeded thanks to the quantitative conception of space, thanks to the idea of numerical relations, thanks to the idea of truth. Now it is not a matter at all of denying these ideas. Here also we must maintain the problematic character of the solution. The certitude of science also poses a problem. These numerical relations are the skeleton of reality perhaps, but the skeleton is not the flesh (although it is necessary for the flesh). It is also necessary to take into account the fact that science is more and more coming to see that the skeleton without the flesh is not even the skeleton. We must also realize that if we were merely skeleton, all reality would be for us a skeleton. (This is the way I am translating the classic phrase: if we were merely mind, all reality would be for us mind.) The idea of a scale must also be acknowledged. At a certain level, we grab onto regularities; but a little above or a little below, we grasp them much less. And yet, the real is at all stages of the scale.

It is perhaps even here where things become things and are con-glomerated into masses, as it is here where they are decomposed in complete juxtaposition.

Is it not that "science" finally becomes aware of this? Some, who hold tightly onto the idea of determinism, are led by their prejudgment to doubt in a profound and lasting way the idea of individuality (in the microscopic); others, seeing that things are neither points nor instan-taneous moments, let determinism drop from their hands, at least in its flat and unilinear form.

A vast collection of studies and analyses would be necessary. Note how space has been conceived in diverse ways by the Chinese (Granet) and the Greeks, by the Gothic and the Baroque. It is something that should be geometricized—or smashed through, pierced—or inflated, dug out. I mean to invoke the space of Cézanne with its distances, its dark iridescences, its transitions.

We would have to see the diverse ideas out of which the idea of space is made: the insubstantial idea from the outside, the ideas of distance, orientation, envelopment. None of these ideas is necessarily implied by any other.

One is not ever very quickly finished with an idea . . .

———————

I cannot help thinking that these reflections call attention to the deca-dence of philosophy. It is curious since the idea of decadence has a stronger grip on me than the idea of progress. "Paradise is behind us." (I have always been afraid of having lost some idea that I could never find again. It is as if someone is saying: "I am doing less and less well.") (But this is no longer absolutely precise—neither for myself, nor for the world. It is going so poorly that I am beginning to believe in progress.)[1]

———————

1. [The last sentence from this parenthesis more than recalls the first line of an unpublished poem of Wahl's (date of composition unknown), "L'esprit de droiture" (perhaps "Spirit of Rectitude"): "Les choses vont si mal que je crois au progrès." The entire poem is found in Barbara Wahl's article in homage to her father's legacy, "Autour de Jean Wahl: Textes, traces, témoignages," *Rivista di storia della filosofia* 3 (2011): 517–38.]

Here things are equally easy for the Marxist, Thomist, and Critical Idealist. They call me petty bourgeois, unbeliever, realist. They speak of a philosophy or poetry of despair even though it is completely the reverse.

I refuse their interpretation, or rather, I accept it. Man's state is divided and problematic. At this end of civilization we are closer than ever to the essence of man (closer than we were under the domination of Catholicism or Stalin or classical thought). It is man who appears pure-impure, attached to the earth, to mysterious influences, miserable, happy in his misery, joyful in his boredom, pitiful: the spectacular, tiny beast.

Seeing things, each apart from the others, seeing things in others: these are the two modes of contemplation of the universe. The first is tied to objectivity; the second to subjectivity. Subjectivity, totality, interiority—objectivity, partiality, exteriority!

We could wonder whether the idea of space will not come to be identified with a more general idea, the idea of alterity. But one could also wonder if in one way or another the idea of alterity, at least in the strong sense of the term, does not assume the idea of space. Here we encounter anew the problems of the interiority of relations and the principle of indiscernibles.

At the moment when the idea of *alterum* is transformed into the idea of *juxta* the idea of space is born—if it is not already contained in the idea of *alterum*.

From here we would be led to take a look at the relations between the idea of space and of cause and substance, in order to see how spatiality is necessary to all our essential ideas—but also to add that this is not necessarily a completely intellectual spatiality, but this primitive, irreducible spatiality to which Kant has so profoundly drawn attention, and which, once attention is drawn to it, actually exceeds Kantianism and its theory of the separation of form and matter, of understanding and intuition.

———————

Perhaps it is best to refuse to pose the problem of time. There are only *problems* of time.

Time, like space, is one of the general, abstract ideas that Berkeley so rightly combated.

There is time in the sense of before and after; there is time in the sense of "at the same time as" [*en même temps que*].

Time could be defined as the fact that nothing happens at the same time—if this assertion does not assume the definition of time, on the one hand, and exclude the "*en même temps*," on the other.

It is also a way to cope with the principle of [non]contradiction.

Everything is not finite in this moment; I can peer ahead and behind, beyond the moment and in it, discerning the before and behind.

Hence the plurality of times and the nonfinite character of time, whether it be the time of things or of thought. Problem: does time derive from the dialectic, or does the dialectic derive from time? In reality, the dialectic presumes time and time makes itself felt by a kind of dialectic.

From this idea of the plurality of times we can pass to the idea of time no longer as idea but as feeling. Behind the "already" and the "not yet" we will find memory and expectation, and behind memory and expectation, we will find remorse and regret, desire and fear. Here we reach what can be called the existential basis of time.

So that which can be touched by the dialectic of thought on the one hand, can also be touched by observing feeling on the other hand.

At the root of time do we not find presupposed (more or less rightly) the idea of truth and falsity on the one hand, and good and evil on the other?

My empiricism, which intends to be radical, like that of James, does not refuse the same consequences, or better, the same presuppositions. We are left to wonder if later it will not be a matter of destroying them. (Later, with time.)

———

I find that the following line of verse expresses one of my most satisfying and simultaneously unsatisfying ideas: "we are in time like a fish in water."

But the fish is not composed of water, and, in a sense, we are not merely composed of time.

I have spoken of the kinship, perhaps the identity of dialectic and time. But there is something, there are even some things that are beyond the dialectic and time. The least of our judgments, in a sense, rise above time, as do, even more, the least of our perceptions. Here there are a multitude of little eternities thought and lived in certain—privileged—fragments of time. These are, *in a sense*, condensations of duration (see Bergson's theory).

Moreover, there are impoverished eternities, like those of the school of Brentano—so very interesting—those reifying thinkers who insist on the region of past facts, on the "it is true that." And there are rich eternities. Or rather: there are dead or dying eternities and living eternities.

The theory of the discontinuity of time is often found tied to a theory of the exteriority of relations (explicated by Russell) and to a theory of the possible. But it would be necessary to study the value of these presuppositions. This idea of the discontinuity of time is today found in certain forms of quantum theory and in the conceptions of Whitehead. Like James, Whitehead conceives of a time that is at once compacted and discontinuous.

In Descartes, the idea of discontinuity, thanks to the idea of the instant, is tied to a certain conception of eternity. Or rather, it assumes this conception of eternity.

Today I realize that this idea of the instant is only an *ersatz* of the idea of eternity, a phantom.

Yet perhaps we attain the instant in certain moments of unconsciousness. As soon as we think it, it no longer exists.

And the instant that I think is already far away.

On Descartes

In order to study more easily the nature of the idea in Descartes, we can distinguish its relations to the mind and the object.

Its relation to the mind provides what Descartes calls the formal reality of the idea (and, at least in one text, it is the same thing that he intends by the material substrate of the idea).

Descartes understands its relation to the object in two very different ways: sometimes the object itself, as it is in the mind, is conceived as being the objective reality of the idea. Sometimes this objective reality is conceived as being the representation, the image of the object. The first theory gives rise to the thought of Arnauld, as well as to Berkeley. The second is that of Malebranche.

On one hand the idea of the object is the object itself (this is the view of James, Bergson, the empirio-criticists, and the neorealists). On the other hand the idea is separated from the object (this is the idea of intentionality in phenomenology and the American critical realists).

It is not easy to sacrifice one of these conceptions for the other: such is the antinomy of realism.

Antinomy, of course, does not mean falsity.

It is even one of the grandeurs of Descartes, the "father of modern idealism," to have expressed the two fundamental and antinomical conceptions of realism.

———

With Maritain I do not consider it just to accuse Descartes of having invented a doctrine of idea-images.

The idea of the sun is not the visible sun; it is the sun of the astronomers, which is drawn from the consideration of innate ideas. The clear and distinct idea is the innate idea.

On the separation and union of the soul and body in Descartes: it has not been sufficiently said that both are demonstrated in the same way. By the faculties: intellection proves the distinction; sensation and imagination prove the union. By nature: the soul is indivisible; matter is divisible (this proves the distinction); yet the soul is indivisible and the body is indivisible (this allows the union). And both are operated by the power of God: God can separate what is distinct, and the same God can unite what is distinct. The God who separates what is distinct is God as the foundation for and the means toward the in-depth exploration of clarity and distinction. The God who unites what is separated is the God who wants to realize a complete man, a being in itself, through uniting the substances, complete in themselves, that are extension and thought.

And just as experience gives the essences as well as this intellectual experience that is the vision of clear and distinct ideas, it cannot be said that the union is demonstrated any less firmly than the distinction. The proof is that experience truly gives a substance—a third substance which comes to be added onto the two clear and distinct ideas of the soul and extension.

As he unites, God creates a separated substance.

Descartes is so strongly in favor of separations that, even when he represents a union, he insists on the fact that this union is not a distinct idea without doubt, but an idea distinguished from what he composes.

———

Of the three kinds of ideas distinguished by Descartes, the ones that are innate in us allow us to escape from ourselves.

Here the idea and judgment are hardly separated any longer. An innate idea is a judgment. "It is virtually the same thing to conceive the idea of God and to conceive that he exists."

Descartes's tendency is doubtlessly to reduce the efficient cause to the formal cause, *causa sive ratio*, to see the idea of cause as being equally applicable to the nontemporal as the temporal (idea of the *causa sui*). This is why he will be able to apply the principle of causality to the ideas. In appearance, Descartes seeks for the cause of the image; in reality, he seeks the reason of the idea.

But he well knows that the efficient cause is not exactly the formal cause. It can simply be treated as the formal cause, in the same way as the formal cause can be treated as an efficient cause (*causa sui*).

Concerning the meeting of the tendencies to fuse notions and to separate notions: these give rise to certain ideas proper to Descartes: in the *Regulae*, the idea that the simple natures can confine relations, and later the idea of the third substance and the idea of continuous creation.

Descartes wants to melt the past, present, and future into this instant where the mind will possess the truth without reasoning, but he also wants to mark a certain distance between things, to stretch them out; this distension is the space that makes the idea in us only like an image of things, and a trace of God, and makes the efficient cause to be never like a quasi-formal cause.

Poetry and Metaphysics

It seems to me that there is something forbidden, something sacrilegious about speaking of the relationship of poetry and metaphysics.[1] Ideas flee when I try to clarify them, rather like those dream images that we would like to preserve. The more we try to secure them, the more quickly they escape us.

In fact, poetry, as Schelling said, is a union of consciousness and unconsciousness, of the subjective and objective. How do we make conscious what involves so many unconscious elements, and objective what involves so many subjective elements?

I am speaking of a certain kind of poetry above all, but perhaps it will allow us to reach the idea, the essence of poetry. Can it shed some

1. The task is facilitated by studies of poetry. Father Brémond moves it closer to mysticism. Others have dealt with this subject in depth from the side of the poetical-metaphysical relationship: Saurat, Rolland de Renéville, Claude-Louis Estève. In the same way Raymond was engaged in exploring contemporary French poetry and Béguin in considering the relation of German Romanticism and metaphysics. Cf. also the books and articles of Maritain and de Corte, where the question is envisaged with the help of an Aristotelian conceptuality, albeit—despite Maritain's possession of a real poetic sense and valuable human sense—without this conceptuality allowing him to offer any new ideas.

I leave Eastern poetry to the side, which would be important to consider. But I think that everything it can teach us is perhaps more rarely but no less intensely found in Western poetry.

light on the relationship that even the poems of the least metaphysical of poets maintain with metaphysics?

It could be said that even today poetry and metaphysics deal with the same subjects but with different techniques. But both poetry and metaphysics try to get rid of every technique. The few masters that we would love to follow do not give a teaching properly speaking. Rimbaud or Mallarmé for poetry and Kierkegaard for the theory of existence are not teaching some or other thing, but teach us to draw out of ourselves things that are difficult to express. Very often we can have the impression today that poetry and metaphysics are at an impasse.

At a certain time they were very deeply united. The Greek sophists very readily relied on Homer and discovered in him the idea of a perpetual transformation of things. Before them the first philosophers were very often poets. Regarding Anaximander we possess the account of Theophrastus: "And things return to where they came, in accordance with what is. For they are given reparation and pay the price for their injustice to each other according to set times." Theophrastus adds: "As Anaximander said in rather poetical terms."[2]

Parmenides formulated his metaphysics in very austere verse. The way of opinion leads us to nothing; those who rely on senses rely on what does not exist. It is necessary to trust only in things that are known by the way of knowledge [*science*]. Thus this poet metaphysician warns us against the poetic universe and lets us open our eyes only to gaze on the brilliance of the eternal sphere of being. Yet the writer of prose, Heraclitus has highlighted the unreasonable elements of the universe—all the while insisting on the logos, a reason, that unites them in a mysterious way.

2. [Fragment 12 B 1, Hermann Diels and Walther Kranz, *Die Fragmente der Vorsokratiker*, 10th ed. (Berlin: Weidmann, 1952). Also found later in Simplicius, *Commentary on the* Physics 24, 17–23. Jonathan Barnes (*Early Greek Philosophy*, 2nd ed. [Oxford: Oxford University Press, 2001], 21) translates the fragment (from Simplicius's use of Theophrastus) in the following way: "And all things from which existing things come into being are also the things into which they are destroyed, in accordance with what must be. For they give justice and reparation to one another for their injustice in accordance with the ordering of time. (He speaks of them in this way in somewhat poetical words)."]

Plato is the heir of these two philosophers. He severely criticizes the poets, Homer and Hesiod. Yet it is Platonism that has for many long centuries made possible the majority of poetic breakthroughs toward metaphysics.

I would like to see what metaphysical patterns poetry can contain, how poetry can give access to the metaphysical world and how the poet sets out from these metaphysical patterns in order to constitute a poetic system.[3]

Whitehead tells us that we must appeal to the witness of the great poets without ceasing. "Their survival is the evidence that they express deep intuitions of mankind penetrating into what is universal in concrete fact."[4] In support of his thesis he cites two examples: Wordsworth and Shelley. In fact, it is perhaps with Romanticism that we see appear most fully the inner relation between poetry and metaphysics. It has been said that Romanticism is the birth and rebirth of wonder: it makes strange things familiar and familiar things strange.[5] Its essence is uncovered in a poet like Novalis when he ceaselessly places his hero before things that he seems to have always known, and which, at the same time—by a singular paradox and essential antinomy—are things that he knows he has never seen. The magic of Novalis can bring before Henry of Ofterdingen, as before the novices at Sais, and before us, a new absolute, which is at the same time very old, a radically foreign element which is at the same time intimately our own.

If we take the problems of memory and time and read Musset's *Souvenir*, the *Tristesse d'Olympio*[6] and the *Lac*,[7] we find this idea of the sacred character of memory that one preserves within himself, and in

3. This is not undertaken without some danger because I risk transforming what is essentially nonconceptual into a concept.

4. [Alfred North Whitehead, *Science in the Modern World* (1925; Cambridge: Cambridge University Press, 2011), 108.]

5. Shelley, and Bergson in our day, have defined art as the power of lifting the veil that habit weaves between us and things.

6. [A poem by Victor Hugo, composed in 1837 but published in *Les rayons et les ombres* (1840).]

7. [A poem by Alphonse de Lamartine, from his *Méditations poétiques* (1820).]

Musset this idea (shown in another manner in Shelley's *Adonais*) that every being and every event has its reverberation in Nature, is retained in its heart, even though it no longer exists in us.[8] But the ideas of Nature and Memory are not elaborated here.[9]

It is not the same in Wordsworth or Shelley, both permeated by the Platonic tradition. Wordsworth makes us feel Nature in its immobility and Shelley in its incessant mobility. It is the idea of "endurance," to use Whitehead's word, of duration, of an immobile and dreary duration, but also sometimes nourishing and consoling, that reading Wordsworth births in us, while Shelley shows us Nature in movement and in the reciprocal interpenetration of its forms. There is in him "a feeling for nature as exhibiting entwined prehensive unities, each suffused with modal presences of the others."[10] Here we have a poetic intuition (in a certain degree derived from philosophical intuitions) translated a little barbarically into the language of contemporary philosophy.

If nature is extensively investigated by Wordsworth and Shelley, it seems to me that Novalis and Hölderlin do the same with time. The feelings of the ever new and ever old that are mingled together in Novalis fall under an affective Platonism. He leads us to an instant that is simultaneously eternity. These poets have observed what Baudelaire and Mallarmé perceived in their own way. Is there not in Baudelaire an echo of Platonism found in his theory of correspondences, of the symbol, of that vision of ourselves as "obscure and plaintive mirrors"? Platonism is equally present, perhaps even more acutely, in Mallarmé,

8. [Wahl seems to refer implicitly to Anatole France's collection, *Les poèmes de souvenir* (1910), which contains the very three poems he invokes here. Literary critic Charles Saint-Beuve had already compared these poems in the previous century.]

9. It would be appropriate to mention the objection of Leconte de Lisle, "What is all that which is not eternal?" and of Vigny, "Love what will never be seen twice." The thought of these two poets is found reconciled to a degree by Novalis or Nietzsche's eternal return.

10. Whitehead. [*Science in the Modern World*, 104. Wahl seems to misquote Whitehead here, for in the latter the reference is clearly to Wordsworth (*The Prelude*, bk. 1), although Whitehead in fact notes two pages later that "Shelley is entirely at one with Wordsworth as to the interfusing of the Presence in nature" (106).]

where the idea appears both as "glory of long . . . desire" and as being "himself at last."[11]

This idea of the instant is found in Blake. He attempts to show us eternity and its presence at each instant of our lives.[12] The role of the poet is to consecrate this moment, to make the passing moment into something that remains and is sanctified by the fact that it is desired, just as the Nietzschean hero wants to maintain it by the notion of the eternal return.

Through this consecration of time, this intensification of the instant, and also by the fact that poetry fills out time in diverse ways (as a magic flight in Shelley or a breathless race as often appears in Swinburne), poetry seems like a manipulation of time.

Regarding space, I will refer again to Blake:

And on its verge the Sun rises and sets, the Clouds bow
To meet the flat Earth and the Sea in such an order'd Space.
The Starry Heavens reach no further, but here bend and set
On all sides, and the two Poles turn on their valves of gold;
And if he moves his dwelling-place, his heavens also move
Where'er he goes, and all his neighbourhood bewail his loss.
Such are the Spaces called Earth and such its dimension.
As to that false appearance, which appears to the reasoner,
As of a Globe rolling thro' the Voidness, it is a delusion of Ulro.
The microscope knows not of this, nor the Telescope: they alter
The ratio of the Spectator's Organs, but leave Objects untouch'd
For every Space larger than a red Globule of Man's blood
Is visionary, and is created by the Hammer of Los.[13]

11. [From Mallarmé, "Prose" and "The Tomb of Edgar Poe," respectively. See *Collected Poems: A Bilingual Edition* (Los Angeles: University of California Press, 1994), 47, 71.]

12. Is this not analogous with Kierkegaardian repetition?

13. [I leave these with Wahl's punctuation, which varies slightly from the original. Elsewhere Wahl translates Blake into French. See William Blake, *Milton a Poem*, ed. Robert Essick and Joseph Viscomi, in *The Illuminated Books of William Blake*, vol. 5 (Princeton: Princeton University Press, 1998), plate 28: 8–20 (178–79). For the quotations from Blake in this and the next chapter, page numbers in

Space is the child of time, the unity that measures change, and it is limited. True space is not the one considered by science but the space that we feel. And its true rhythm and principle are located in its smallest fragment, in the same way as the principle of time was found in its smallest fragment, the instant.

There is found in Blake what we could call a concrete notion of space and time. This is approached in contemporary poetry by Claudel, who, in his *Art poétique*, sketched his own philosophy. He expounded on his idea of causality, the pressure things exert on each other. He speaks of knowledge as something elementary, of which human knowledge is only the final efflorescence. "Blue knows the color orange, truly the hand knows its shadow on the wall." Knowledge is a compresence, as Alexander said, a first juxtaposition of subject and object, and since we are here before the idea of knowledge, I return to a poem of Traherne, leaving Romantic poetry but not the poetry of astonishment:

> My naked simple life was I.
> That Act so strongly shin'd,
> Upon the Earth, the Sea, the Sky,
> It was the substance of the Mind.
> The sense its self was I.
> I felt no Dross nor Matter in my Soul,
> No Brims nor Borders, such as in a Bowl
> We see: My Essence was *Capacity*.
> . . . .
> This made me present evermore
> With whatsoere I saw.
> . . . .
> There was my Sight, my Life, my Sense,
> My Substance, ev'n my Mind.
> My Spirit shin'd
> Ev'n there, not by a *transeunt* Influence.
> The Act was immanent, yet *there*,

---

parentheses refer to the Princeton edition of *The Illuminated Books* unless otherwise noted.]

The Thing remote, yet felt ev'n *here*.
O Joy! O Wonder and Delight!
O sacred Mystery![14]

What can the poets say about the unknowable?[15] In 1796 Hegel dedicated a poem to Hölderlin:

Dank dir, du meine
Befreierin o Nacht!
. . . .
Der Sinn verliert sich in dem Anschaun,
was mein ich nannte schwindet,
ich gebe mich dem Unermesslichen dahin.
Ich bin in ihm, bin alles, bin nur es.
Dem wiederkehrenden Gedanken fremdet,
ihm graut vor dem Unendlichen, und staunend fasst
er dieses Anschauns Tiefe nichte.
. . . .
Dem Sohn der Weihe war der hohen Lehren Fülle
des unaussprechlichen Gefühles Tiefe viel zu heilig,
als dass er trockne Zeichen ihrer würdigte.
Schon der Gedanke fasst die Seele nicht,
die ausser Zeit und Raum in Ahndung der Unendlichkeit

versunken, sich vergisst, und wieder zum Bewusstsein nun
erwacht. Wer gar davon zu andern sprechen wollte,
spräch er mit Engelzungen, fühlt der Worte Armuth;
ihm graut das Heilige so klein gedacht,
durch sie so klein gemacht zu haben, dass die Red' ihm Sünde
    deucht,

14. ["My Spirit," Thomas Traherne, *Selected Poems and Prose* (New York: Penguin Classics, 1992).]
15. Here we would have to take up the much too massive subject of the link between love and metaphysics as it is suggested in Shelley's *Epipsychidion* or Wagner's *Tristan*, for example.

und dass er bebend sich den Mund verschliesst.
Was der Geweihte sich so selbst verbot, verbot ein weises
Gesetz den ärmern Geistern; das nicht kund zu tun,
was er in heil'ger Nacht geseh'n, gehört, gefühlt . . .

Thanks be to you, you my
liberator, oh night!
. . . .
sense shedding itself in intuition,
what I call mine fading,
I give myself to the vastness therein,
I am in it, am everything, am only it.
recurring reflection becomes alien,
it dreads before infinity, and astonished grasps
not the depth of this intuition.
. . . .
To the son of the initiation was the richness of the high learning
the unexpressable [sic] feeling's depth much too holy
than that he should value their dull signs.
Even the thought does not seize the soul
which outside of Time and Space lost in premonition of infinity
forgets itself and again to consciousness now
awakens. Whosoever would wish to speak thereof to others,
speaks he with tongues of angels, feeling the poverty of the
        words;
he dreads the holy so little contemplated,
through words to have been made so small, that speech to him
        seems sin,
and that he, shaking, closes his mouth.
What the initiated thus himself forbade, forbade a wise
law the poorer spirits to make known
what he on the holy night saw, heard, felt . . .

("Eleusis," to Hölderlin, August 1796)[16]

16. [I quote Alan W. Grose's English translation of Hegel's "Eleusis," *The Philosophical Forum* 33, no. 3 (2002): 312–17.]

In this poetry we see asserted the pantheist mysticism of the young Hegel. It had been thought that Hegel did not like this infinite that terrified his thought. But still, he is plunged into it like Hölderlin and Novalis. For them all that is thought is attached to the unthinkable, as all that is visible to the invisible, and all that one understands to what cannot be understood.[17]

The junction of poetry and metaphysics is accomplished below, on the one hand, and above, on the other. If there is a metaphysical base, a hypophysical domain—that which Nietzsche, Whitman, Lawrence, Boehme, and Schelling wanted to draw out—if there is a massive torpor at the root of nature and sometimes at our root, it is precisely there that a junction between poetry and metaphysics can be found. And on the other hand, if there is a point toward which metaphysics tends—like an arch reaching toward its summit—then here also this link can be found, for that of which the philosopher senses the power can be indicated only by something other than discourse, and this "something other" can be poetry. There would therefore be a block of the real and of acute moments, there would be the base and summit of the pyramid, and it is by this immense base and acute summit that the communication would be realized between the two domains we are studying.

If we return to the hypotheses examined by Plato in the *Parmenides*—first, that the one is only one and disappears in order to become a sort of nonbeing, and then, that the one is all—then we could find in the *Illuminations* and the *Saison en enfer* the equivalent of the chaos of the second hypothesis and the equivalent of the negative

---

17. The poet has been placed in opposition to the mystic. The mystic was preferred. This is perhaps unjust. They say the poet speaks and the mystic remains silent. But the mystics have indeed spoken, at length, saying again what other mystics said before them. And the poets have indeed been aware that the most valuable moment of their poem is when it falls into silence; it is the sound that is extinguished little by little, and finally its empty form vanishes, of which the memory, by moments of silence, renders again more sacred than the poem, melodious thanks to the poem, before being itself absolute silence. There is a complex dialectic in the poem, a dialogue of dialogue with the silence that engulfs it and causes it to come alive again.

theology of the first. The poet is the one who is aware of all this disorder of being and of this purity of nonbeing spoken of by Valéry.

But between these two domains through which poetry and metaphysics could perhaps be united, there are a great number of regions of the soul where this junction could likewise be brought about. The human soul knows many lands, and they are its own. This notion of regions through which the soul, the I, passes is on display in Blake. It is the theory of *states*. There is nothing real about the I; what is real are the states that it traverses.[18]

Poetry causes us to know what is most subjective under the most universal aspect. We can ask ourselves whether what we find at the root of poetry are not the great types of being that Plato's reflection has uncovered. Thibaudet shows that when Valéry attempts to know himself he only sees nonbeing (and, we could add, its "possibilities"), and when he creates he sees being forming before him. In him there is a nihilism of knowledge and a positivism of creation. If we then comprehend every movement of philosophical thought from Parmenides to Mallarmé and Valéry, we see that this nonbeing and these possibles that Parmenides excluded are, on the contrary, precisely what—in a sense—captures the gaze of Mallarmé and Valéry. Nothingness, that which is absolutely not, the blankness of the page and the darkness of the night of the *Igitur*, the fate that cannot be abolished: these are among the dominant themes of Mallarmé's poetry. The possible that was expelled from Parmenides's poem found a place in the universe of Valéry—and in such a way that we find a reflection on being and nonbeing both in these metaphysical poets and in this poet metaphysician. But the poets arrive at their conclusions by a completely different way than the philosopher. Here we conceive the possibility even of a poetry of being. Claudel and Whitman perhaps give us some idea.

---

18. In Nietzsche a plastic equivalent of this theory can be found in the description of landscapes, categorizable as heroic, idyllic, and heroic-idyllic. Perhaps it could even be said that tragedy, idyll, elegy, and all the great classical genres are only attempts to translate the different states of the soul into well-defined genres that correspond to them.

The idea of the Same explicates the feeling of Unity, and its role in poetry is difficult to overemphasize since it is present in the love of nature, in the love of the other self, in the love of God, and we find it at the bottom of that cult of the Night which constitutes one of the principal chapters of the book of Rolland de Renéville. Novalis, Nerval, Wagner, Baudelaire have all celebrated Unity under the dark spaces of the Night.

One could show the importance of the idea of the Other as that of a call toward the other, toward a felt presence and as an affirmation of things and beings that we cannot reach—and in such a way that it would be necessary to distinguish profoundly between the alterity that calls to us, to which we pray (whether that of a human person or god), and the alterity before which we are threatened (whether the object of a negative ontology, the god of a negative theology or another I, cruel and closed off). If we now consider the Same and Other, no longer as isolated but as united, the play of the Same and Other, and the influence of the Same on the Other, do we not find the Platonic idea of participation and all its derivatives: correspondence, symbol, image, reflections, analogies, Platonic love? Is it not precisely because Plato has put his hand on this mechanism of the Same in the Other that he stands at the origin of this poetic Platonism?

After the same and the other, we could cite the two last categories that, for the Plato of the *Sophist*, complete the hierarchy of great categories: movement and rest. We have already spoken of these in relation to Wordsworth and Shelley.

How are all the categories united by the poet? How are they bound together and how are they opposed? By the play of analogies and antitheses. The analogies are the "correspondences" of Baudelaire. The antitheses are described by Blake: "A Negation is not a Contrary; Contraries are Positives. . . . Two contraries are positives to each other."[19] And these analogies and antitheses will come to dissolve before our eyes if we recall the mystical experiences of Novalis or Nerval, "The Marriage of the Seasons" in Novalis, the fusion of the Virgin and the Cybil in Nerval, or of Christ and Dionysos in Hölderlin, the eternal

19. [*Milton a Poem*, bk. II (title), plate 30 (181).]

return when "the thirteenth comes back" in Nerval, or when the "great noon" sounds in Nietzsche.

The discernible danger in these concurrences between metaphysicians and poets is that the themes of poetry would become conceptualized. To consider these themes independently of the way in which they are incorporated in the texts is to consider them wrongly.

From this vantage it would be interesting to study the connections between a poet like Hölderlin and a philosopher like Hegel. The thesis could be sustained that they are starting from experiences that are nearly identical. But what became the great philosophy of Hegel—transformed by another temperament—became the poetry of Hölderlin. Therefore we do not say that the poet is a failed metaphysician. Nor do we say that the metaphysician is a failed poet. Idealism is not the philosophy of a poet, and German Romanticism is not the poetry of a philosopher. Moreover it is doubtful that one could travel any further into the regions of metaphysics by means of poetry than by some other means of expression, such as drawing, color, or the sound of music, for metaphysics is in the last analysis nothing conceptual at all. The strokes of Rembrandt or the colors of El Greco do not arouse in us thoughts any less spiritually metaphysical than a poem by Vigny or Coventry Patmore. Rest is better known in its essence, in an essence even more reposed, by Cézanne than by Wordsworth, and movement, billowing forth (as it were) in its essence, is better known by Van Gogh than by Shelley.[20]

The way that poetry incarnates its idea is different from that of a system of philosophy. Hölderlin tries to determine this indeterminable that he has before his eyes in a poem he composed as a letter: "Storms, not just their greatest manifestation, but seen as power and figure, among the other forms of the sky, the effect of the light, shaping nationally and as a principle and destiny, so that something is holy to us, the intensity of its coming and going, the characteristicness of the woods and the coincidence in one region of different characters of

20. Repeating an idea of Plato, we could say that the poet is four steps from reality, whereas the painter or sculptor is only three. Yet perhaps this very distance that he finds himself from the real permits him a better approach to it, or at least an approach to its essence that is more intelligible.

nature, so that all the holy places of the earth are together in one place, and the philosophic light at my window, they are now my joy."[21]

Thus the instant will be for the poet the essence of his reflection, bathed in however a philosophical a light.

A little later, Hölderlin wrote:

In lovely blue the steeple blossoms
With its metal roof. Around which
Drift swallow cries, around which
Lies most loving blue. The sun,
High overhead, tints the roof tin,
But up in the wind, silent,
The weathercock, crows.[22]

There is nothing metaphysical in this poem, properly speaking. But the emotion that it invokes causes this instant to be separated from every other and lived intensely; at once so familiar and so strange, it allows us to divine the veiled face of that which Hölderlin calls the philosophical light.[23]

The same Hölderlin says, "A sign we are, without meaning."[24] And it is this sense of the absence of sense that his poem brings to us, along with the feeling that we are here without knowing why, but still that this instant is somehow consecrated by the very fact that we are living it.

Baudelaire writes: "In certain nearly supernatural states of the soul, the profundity of life reveals itself whole and entire in the sight before one's eyes, however ordinary it may be. There it becomes a symbol."[25] It is in this way that every great poem is susceptible to metaphysical signification, even if it does not contain anything metaphysical itself.

21. [Friedrich Hölderlin, Letter 110, *Essays and Letters*, ed. Jeremy Adler and Charlie Louth (New York: Penguin, 2009), 214.]

22. [Hölderlin, "In lovely blue . . . ," *Hymns and Fragments*, trans. Richard Sieburth (Princeton: Princeton University Press, 1984), 249.]

23. Every passion is a charm, says Novalis. The passion of Orpheus stands at the origin of order itself and its construction. And its sorrow.

24. [Hölderlin, "Mnemosyne," *Hymns and Fragments*, 117.]

25. [Baudelaire, *Oeuvres complètes*, vol. 1 (Paris: Gallimard, 1975), 287.]

Keats's *Ode on a Grecian Urn*, Hugo's *Sur une Stèle antique*, even such a poem of Chénier, such a tragedy of Racine, where the sea of passions is contained in the play of rhymes and the unity of day and place, such a drama of Shakespeare, such a *Dinggedicht* of Rilke, arouse the worlds of metaphysical thought, awakening in their virtual hearth a blinding eruption of unthought thoughts and almost unformulatable formulae.[26]

The very description of what is given to us in reality can include a philosophical signification.

Poetry will be a union of contradictories, for what cannot be imagined will be presented under the form of images which often—as Bergson has shown—are followed in order to be destroyed, finally giving forth the idea of that which is no longer an image. Pure quality will be presented under the form of quantity. Words will be endowed simultaneously with a "purer sense" and more impure sense, and in these two ways they will be distinguished from our ordinary words.

It is yet by this union of things that contradict one another that the poet will not only be able to lead us to the beyond, but, once we have perceived this beyond, leads us back toward the here below, joining immanence to transcendence. Heidegger taught this by his notion of "belonging to the earth" through reference to Hölderlin.

The poet will make us feel that the physical is the metaphysical and that which passes by is eternal.[27] Here Novalis, Rimbaud, Whitman, and Nietzsche agree.

26. Blake writes [*Milton a Poem*, plate 27: 1–7 (176)]:

Some Sons of Los surround the Passions with porches of iron & silver
Creating form & beauty around the dark regions of sorrow.
Giving to airy nothing a name and a habitation
Delightful: with bounds of the Infinite putting off the Indefinite
Into most holy forms of Thought: (such is the power of inspiration)
They labour incessant; with many tears & afflictions:
Creating the beautiful House for the piteous sufferer.

27. The poet does not appeal to the same region of ourselves as the writer of prose. He disturbs an interior lake that mysteriously communicates with the ocean, which the Greeks conceived as the origin of all things. It was none other than Schelling who sought to define it: the union of the subjective and objective. [The poet] touches extreme subjectivity and by that joins us to the cosmos.

"Eternity is the sea gone with the sun," said Rimbaud.[28] Nietzsche said it is the Noontime of Joy. In these contradictories that we see at play, in this union of transcendence and immanence, we equally discover the explication of the fact that the poet is at once subject and object, subjective and objective, conscious and unconscious, active and passive—and living these contradictions in a tension, in an intensity that is lyricism. Here we are *not* merely rediscovering Heraclitus's ancient thought about "the harmony of opposed tensions like that of the lyre." Modern poetry is distinguished from ancient poetry by its subjectivity, by this lyrical subjectivity that began to develop with Romanticism. There is doubtlessly something there essential to all poetry. If, apparently, Lucretius worked with the most objective concepts in order to constitute his poem, it is nevertheless the case that his passion was intensified through contact with these very concepts and was expressed with all the more personality as the world before which he found himself was an impersonal world destructive of such passion. The flame aware of its immanent extinguishment only burned all the more strongly in this dark world.

In some way the poet is conscious of the unconscious. "To dream and altogether not to dream, to be in a state of complete wakefulness and yet to dream."[29]

And it is Novalis still who allows us to see the union of activity and passivity. The poet is the one within whom can be known something analogous to what one imagines to be the creative activity of the world; this is the meaning of the word *poet* in full force—the creator, and who is also the one who can write, like Novalis: "One does not create [*fait*], but he does [*fait*] what he can [*faire*]."[30]

And in such a way that the poet will no longer know if it is he who speaks or another. He does not know anymore to whom he is addressed, or for whom he writes. It is for no one other than himself, and it is not for himself.

28. [A variation on the opening and closing lines of "Eternity" quoted earlier.]

29. [Novalis, *Werke* (Munich: Beck, 1969), 433.]

30. Surely Baudelaire intended something analogous when he wrote, "With the vaporization and centralization of the self, all is there." Similarly, Hugo says in a passage cited by Béguin: "The question is to know to what degree the song belongs to the voice and poetry to the poet."

What is he trying to do when what is not addressed to him is addressed to a him who is not he? He is trying to build and destroy at once, to save this moment and to be delivered from it by destroying it. He is the "widowed, the inconsolable," but also the one who is incited toward an audacious endeavor. He carries the unconscious to consciousness. He destroys himself while affirming himself through expression. He is Orpheus resurrecting Eurydice, but under the mask of the maenad who kills him: it is he, he and his poetry, that we recognize.

The manipulation of time, poetry is also the manipulation of ourselves. It is our prayer and our revolt. It is our chance that we seal with the seal of necessity. It is our destiny. The poet is Prometheus the Rebel, Orpheus bringing unconscious Eurydice to the light, Pygmalion blowing his soul into Galatea. He is also Ulysses returning to the country of his birth, Empedocles united to the unleashed forces of nature, the maenads who destroy the poet himself. There is a struggle of metaphysics against poetry and of poetry against metaphysics, yet they always remain bound together, living out of their reciprocal deaths, each being born at the moment of the other's destruction, but also living through their reciprocal lives. When metaphysics is reduced to silence at the root of ourselves, then suddenly poetry raises its voice. But in this voice we hear the echo of a departed metaphysician.

What will be the destiny of the poet today? Hölderlin writes:

But, my friend, we have come too late.
. . . .
. . . and who wants poets at all in lean years?
But they are, as you say, like those holy ones, priests of the wine-god
Who in holy Night roamed from one place to the next.[31]

We can no longer construct great metaphysical poems, and it is perhaps difficult in our day to construct great poems. Better to remain in our place marked by the destiny of our culture and our own specific destiny and to create [faire] what we can [faire], however little it may

31. Hölderlin, "Bread and Wine," *Selected Poems and Fragments*, trans. Michael Hamburger (New York: Penguin Classics, 1998), 157.

be. During the present time of distress, perhaps not a poetry of distress, but a poetry born from it in order to surmount it, after appropriating it. Perhaps in the coming epoch the fundamental intuitions of every domain will become vaguer, more ponderous, more shapeless, whereas the ideas that correspond to them will become finer and more subtle.

What I have said about the relation of poetry and metaphysics evokes in me the feeling that everything has been done [*fait*] by the poets and that everything remains to be done [*faire*] for the sake of the appearing of the metaphysico-poetic Truth.[32] I cite a very short poem that summarizes this relation between poetry and metaphysics. Metaphysics speaks, and says:

> Poetry, elder sister,
> Let your song soar,
> I hear you, and it is I who speak.

We know neither what metaphysics is, nor what poetry is, but the heart of poetry will always be metaphysical, and there is a strong possibility that the heart of metaphysics is equally always poetical.

---

32. All great poetry is simultaneously a surrealism and realism. The error of surrealism properly speaking, or rather, its errors, is to have believed that one could discover the surreal by *mots en liberté* ["stream of consciousness"], and also to have believed oneself to be a surrealist when one was all along practicing post-surrealism (the true surrealists being Blake and Rimbaud). Its permanent glory is found in having maintained in the most violent manner this essence of poetry. The task at hand, today above all, is to forget not what it was, and what its role remains, despite its errors. We remain grateful to it for the non-new truths that it has articulated.

Magic and Romanticism

Notes on Novalis and Blake

No poet has mused with more intensity about magic and its relation to art than Novalis. That he regarded the science of his day and its astonishing discoveries in the domain of electricity and saw the philosophers—Kant, and his idea of synthetic a priori judgments, Fichte, and his theory of the act by which the I is posited and posits the world—to be "truly magical"; that, above all, he observed himself and that delicate organization through which he perceived things simultaneously in their detail and infinity: all this led him to the conception of a universal thaumaturgy. And this constituted his magic idealism by which he surpassed Fichte in Fichteanism and Romanticism in Romanticism. It is the idea of an ennobling and a deepening of things solely by our manner of seeing them in their grandeur and profundity; it is the idea of an art of a priori discovery, modifying the world and our organs, healing our bodies, shaping our perceptions, fashioning our ideas, creating God by our prayer and our faith.

Magic is the art of using the world for our purposes. What are we? Personified and all-powerful points of reality. The individual is a magic principle. He possesses the art of becoming omnipotent, of causing miracles and at the same time of seeing everything as a miracle.

This art is a fruit of belief. Mysticism is magic. Here vision, will, and intelligence are united. All our faculties are smelted into one another in the act of intellectual intuition, which Kant negated, but the affirmation of which is the essence of the thought of his successors. Intellectual intuition, says Novalis, is the key to life.

This intuition is irreducible to and incommensurable with reason. The more something is independent of reason, the more it can become the starting point for determination. This is the foundation of magic.

But in this art of transcendental well-being, the poet enjoys a privileged place. He is truly the transcendental doctor.

He operates through words, by conjuring up objects, and these words and objects are a charm, an enchantment.

He operates through words. Every word employed by the poet is an incantation. It does not serve as a sign, but as a tone. He enjoys a magical intuition of objects. He is an enchanter because he is intensely impassioned, and every passion is itself a charm.

He creates a poetic world. Thought is speech and speech is action. In the beginning of the world is the word—or thought—or action. Knowledge and act are identical. All this is one. And all this is identical to love. Love acts magically.

Art is therefore not observation: the beautiful is not given, but created. The vision of the artist moves from the inside out, and not the outside in. The poet is he who puzzles out a priori symphonies and thereby transforms nature.

Heinrich von Ofterdingen brims with these ideas. All of a sudden Henry hears a word that he does not understand, but which nevertheless resonates deeply throughout his entire being. All around him are raised songs that make the world appear at once more familiar and more mysterious, and which open up infinite depths to him. He turns his attention more and more to antiquity when all was poetry, and toward the future when the master of the domain of sounds will perhaps become master of the world. Through contact with the poet nature is allowed to pass into happier, more divine fantasies; nature dances, glides, climbs to heaven. With the poet, nature has a marvellous time.

Poetry is magical thought. There are prophets, magic men, true poets—they romanticize the world. Be always in a state of poetry!

It is appropriate to note that all of these affirmations for Novalis are not the consequences of a priori conceptions. They come from experience. Experience shows us in itself the presence of the a priori, of the magical, of the voluntary. All experience is magical and is only explicable magically.

It should also be noted, following the dialectic of Novalis's thought, that, limiting itself, sometimes negating itself, it is not necessary to concede too much to magic (if grossly conceived), to poetry, or to action. Do not concede too much to pure magic for it is through laziness that man demands pure magic, as if it were sheer mechanics. Do not cede too much to poetry. For among the arts, poetry plays the role that prose plays in relation to poetry: it is the most prosaic of arts. Whether we compare it to painting, to music, to this world, and to silence.

Do not cede too much to pure action. The same Novalis who writes in a delightfully clumsy French, "Il est beaucoup plus commode d'être fait que de se faire lui-même" (It is much more fitting to be created than to create oneself), and who wants to see man *en état de créateur absolu* (in a state of absolute creativity), is also the one who says: "La jouissance et le laisser-faire ont beaucoup plus de prix qu'on ne le croit d'ordinaire. La passivité est souvent bien plus haute que l'activité. Toute activité cesse quand arrive le vrai savoir, le grand savoir" (Ecstatic pleasure and leaving things be have a much higher value than is ordinarily believed. Passivity is often much higher than activity. Every activity ceases on the arrival of true knowledge, the great knowledge). And once again in French: "On ne fait pas, mais on fait qu'il se puisse faire" (One does not create, but does what one can). This is a striking formulation that shows us the poet summoning the self and gathering unknown forces above the self. He is the place of confluence [*rencontre*] among these forces; the place of magical encounter [*rencontre*]. Magic is the extreme of activity that is overturned and becomes the extreme of passivity.

———————

A meditation on magic is not found in Blake as it is in Novalis. And yet their thinking is very close. Blake's theory of imagination is, though distinctly accented, the very theory of Novalis. The "first principle" of Blake is that the "Poetic Genius is the true Man, and that the body or outward form of Man is derived from the Poetic Genius."[1] In 1820 he repeats what he wrote in 1788: "The eternal body of man is The IMAGINATION, that is God himself, the Divine Body . . . JESUS. We are his Members. It manifests itself in his Works of Art. (In Eternity All is Vision.)"[2] And again: "Art is the Tree of Life. Science is the Tree of Death. GOD is Jesus. The world of Imagination is the World of Eternity it is the Divine bosom into which we shall go after the death of the Vegetated body."[3]

It is the same thinking that explains this passage from *Milton*:

And of the sports of wisdom in the human imagination
Which is the Divine Body of the Lord Jesus, blessed for ever.
. . . .
According to the inspiration of the Poetic Genius
Who is the eternal all-protecting Divine Humanity,
To whom be Glory and Power and Dominion Evermore. Amen.[4]

All things exist within the human imagination, Blake writes in *Jerusalem*.

And he embodies the "Four Faces of Humanity . . . [that] conversed together in Visionary Forms dramatic, which bright redounded from their Tongues in thunderous majesty, in Visions, in new Expanses, creating exemplars of Memory and of Intellect: Creating Space, Creating Time according to the wonders Divine of Human Imagination."[5]

1. [*All Religions are One, The Complete Poetry and Prose of William Blake*, ed. David V. Erdman (Berkeley: University of California Press, 2008), 1–2.]

2. [*Laocoön, The Complete Poetry and Prose of William Blake*, 272–73.]

3. [Ibid., 274. (Wahl inverts the order of the first two sentences.) *A Vision of the Last Judgment, Complete Poetry and Prose of William Blake*, 555. (Wahl quotes these two passages as if from the same text.)]

4. [*Milton a Poem*, ed. Robert Essick and Joseph Viscomi, in *The Illuminated Books of William Blake*, vol. 5 (Princeton: Princeton University Press, 1998), plate 2(b): 3–4 (114), plate 12: 1–3 (137).]

5. [William Blake, *Jerusalem: The Emanation of the Giant Albion*, ed. Morton Paley, in *The Illuminated Books of William Blake*, vol. 1 (Princeton: Princeton University Press, 1998), plate 98: 26–32 (294). I follow Wahl in ignoring the poetic line breaks here and elsewhere below when quoting the text in line.]

The poet is the man of imagination as well as the man of desire. And he becomes Albion (the universal man) whose paths are ideas of the imagination.

> As the breath of the Almighty, such are words of man to man
> In the great Wars of Eternity, in fury of Poetic Inspiration
> To build the Universe stupendous: Mental forms Creating
> . . . .
> The Human Imagination which is the Divine Vision and Fruition.[6]

This imagination is not a state but human existence itself.

The enemies of the imagination are Blake's enemies. And these enemies are the moral law.

> O human imagination, O divine body that I have crucified
> I turned my back on you, concerning myself with the deserts of
>   the moral law.

And it is reasoning, abstract philosophy, that wages war against the imagination.

And it is the imitation of nature.

If one turns away from morality, from reason, and from the enslaved observation of the real, everything from that moment on reveals its infinity. The gates of each instant and at each point turn on their hinges.

> . . . within that Center Eternity expands
> Its ever during doors . . .[7]

One must open "the Eternal Worlds . . . the immortal Eyes of Man inwards into the Worlds of Thought."[8] And, in fact,

6. [Blake, *Milton a Poem*, plate 30: 18–20 (181–82), plate 32: 19–20 (185). Wahl gives no ellipsis between the third and fourth line, although the fourth appears later in the poem. Wahl's French rendering of this line is: "L'imagination humaine est la vision et la jouissance divine."]

7. [*Milton a Poem*, plate 31(34): 48–49 (184).]

8. [*Jerusalem*, plate 5: 18–19 (136).]

The nature of infinity is this! That every thing has its
Own Vortex, and when once a traveller thro Eternity
Has passed that Vortex, he perceives it roll backward behind
His path, into a globe itself infolding: like a sun:
Or, is developing in a globe like a sun
Or like a moon, or like a universe of starry majesty.[9]

The briefest moment is equivalent to the greatest length of time.

Every Time less than a pulsation of the artery
Is equal in its period & value to Six Thousand Years
For in this Period the Poet's Work is Done: and all the Great
Events of Time start forth & are conceived in such a Period
Within a Moment: a Pulsation of the Artery.[10]

Blake never tires of diving into this infinity.

What is above is Within, for everything in Eternity is translucent:
The Circumference is Within: Without is formed the Selfish Center
And the Circumference still expands going forward to Eternity.
And the Center has Eternal States![11]

Here is seen the importance of what Blake calls the *minute particulars*, opposed to the generalities of reason.
Every particular thing is a soul; each is a person.

---

9. [*Milton a Poem*, plate 1: 21–27 (133).]
10. [Ibid., plates 27–28: 62–63; 1–3 (177–78).] Cf. [*Auguries of Innocence*, ll. 1–4]:

> To see a World in a Grain of Sand
> And a Heaven in a Wild Flower
> Hold Infinity in the palm of your hand
> And Eternity in an hour.

[*The Complete Poetry and Prose of William Blake*, 490.]
11. [*Jerusalem*, plate 71: 6–9 (247).]

If our imagination opens up its wings, it will teach us to see the lark as a powerful angel, and every particle of matter as a person.

Each grain of Sand
Every Stone on the Land
Each rock & each hill
Each fountain & rill
Each herb & each tree
Mountain hill Earth & Sea
Cloud Meteor & Star
Are Men Seen Afar[12]

. . . .

My Eyes more & more
Like a Sea without shore
Continue Expanding
The Heavens commanding
Till the Jewels of Light
Heavenly Men beaming bright
Appeard as One Man
Who Complacent began
My limbs to infold
In his beams of bright gold[13]

Ultimately these minute particulars ought to be reunited in the universal man.

12. [Letter 15: 25–32, in *The Complete Poetry and Prose of William Blake*, 712.] Or as he will say in *Jerusalem* [plate 71: 15–19 (247)]:

For all are Men in Eternity. Rivers Mountains Cities Villages.
All are Human & when you enter into their Bosoms you walk
In Heavens & Earths; as in your own Bosom you bear your Heaven
And Earth, & all you behold, tho it appears Without it is Within
In your Imagination . . .

13. [Letter 15: 45–54, in *The Complete Poetry and Prose of William Blake*, 713.]

In Great Eternity, every particular Form gives forth or Emanates
Its own peculiar Light & the Form is the Divine Vision
And the Light is his Garment This is Jerusalem in every Man[14]

And again:

But General Forms have their vitality in Particulars: & every
Particular is a Man; a Divine Member of the Divine Jesus.[15]

And now we reach the conclusion of *Jerusalem*:

All human forms identified even Tree Metal Earth & Stone. all
Human Forms identified. Living . . .[16]

The great magical work of transmutation of metals into gold, the
ambition of the philosopher to unite the particulars and the universal,
in what Hegel will call the idea, we find again in Blake and Novalis,
and Coleridge, when each tells us in turn of the imagination and the
creative *logos*, human and divine.

Could one trace the subterranean currents of thought that run
from the exemplarism of the Middle Ages, and even perhaps from the
Platonic demiurge, to these thinkers? How the idea of creation, passing
from man as creator in order then to climb up to his idea of God, comes
to redescend to man, giving birth to the Romantic conception—this is
a question I leave to others with a desire to examine it. I am convinced
that emerging in many passages from Albert the Great there can be
found already the ideas that will form the essence of Romanticism.

At the end of the eighteenth century, Swedenborg, and later Saint-
Martin, are the direct inheritors of certain currents that stretch back
through the Renaissance to the Middle Ages, alternately coloring the
fiery alcohol stills and the flame of divine love.

14. [*Jerusalem*, plate 54: 1–3 (216).]
15. [Ibid., plate 91: 29–30 (285).]
16. [Ibid., plate 99: 1–2 (296).]

And in the last half of the nineteenth century, Baudelaire, and sometimes Mallarmé, more clearly (but also sometimes oratorically) Villiers de l'Isle-Adam, and finally Rimbaud, take their place in this tradition of magic poetry, a tradition of active and transmutative thinking, a tradition both antimaterialist[17] and revolutionary.

17. If, that is, we give the word *matter* its ordinary sense. We would have to make an exception here in the case of Rimbaud, or for certain moments of his thought. And, moreover, do the words *materialist* and *antimaterialist* conserve any meaning at all, if we become aware of the impossibility of defining matter, either as opposed to the spirit, or as identical with it?

Novalis and the Principle
of Contradiction

When he philosophizes, Novalis, properly speaking, does not seek a solution. "The transformation of one or more propositions into a problem is an ascent. A problem is much more than a proposition" (H. 1090). He wants to awaken our sense of thought, to fluidize our thinking.

Here, above all, I want to show, in a few words, the role that contradiction plays in the life of the mind, according to Novalis.

Without a doubt there are for him purely intellectual contradictions, the value of which uniquely consists in the fact that they bring to ruin the system or the work that leads to them. Thus Wilhelm Meister leads to contradictions because it is written for and by the understanding (B. 360). But there are other fecund contradictions that are essential to the life of the mind.

He writes: "To destroy the principle of contradiction is perhaps the highest task of the highest logic" (H. 578). And indeed, what is

I have designated by Bl. the fragments that belong to the Blütenstaub, by B. the fragments assembled by Bülow, by H. those published for the first time by Heilborn, by Sc. those that Schlegel and Tieck had already provided in their edition of Novalis's works. I have utilized the edition that appeared with Diederichs [*Novalis Schriften*, 4 vols., ed. Jacob Minor], Jena: 1907.

our mind but an instrument of linkage between completely heterogeneous terms? (H. 307).[1] Every synthetic concept contains two concepts opposed to each other (H. 8). We cannot think absolute unity, for it would be void of thinking. The concept of identity must contain in itself the concept of activity, and change. The essence of what we can conceive of higher reality is a unified duality (H. 100). The more the elements [of thought] are heterogeneous, the more the substance will be massive and powerful (H. 445).

There will therefore be life, or, to use the very words of Novalis, animation of thought, only when extremes communicate with one another (B. 385; cf. H. 445). The hallmark of genius is to unite ceaselessly opposed extremes (Bl. 26, 54), which is the work of the faculty that the Romantics term the *Witz*, "principle of affinity, *menstruum universale*" (Bl. 57).

Novalis dreams of man as contradicting himself without end (Bl. 26). He unifies extreme volatility with extreme energy (H. 213), surplus with lack (Bl. 27), nobility with the possibility of being common when one chooses to be (Sc. 296), playfulness with seriousness (which produces expressions like "a gravity that plays about"; "he laughed in an infinitely serious manner": 156, 222; H. 754, 874), melancholy with ecstasy, childhood with wisdom. A fulfilled man is a beautiful satire, in the sense understood by the Latins (H. 487). He is a kind of chaos, but an ordered chaos. He is unlimited; he is given limitations and yet remains boundless.

Consciousness and unconsciousness come to be fused into one another. True thinking is simultaneously thought and nonthought (H. 1100). In the first place Novalis understands, in a Fichtean manner, that thinking is action. But he also means that there are patterns of thought that one should never clearly acknowledge to oneself (Sc. 40). In this way he examines in a number of fragments what we would today call narcissism or introversion. One should ceaselessly remain at the boundary of consciousness and unconsciousness.

---

1. Similar ideas are found in the writings of the young Hölderlin, and, obviously, in Hegel. They are related to some ideas of Fichte and even Kant.

"To dream and not to dream at once—synthesized—the activity of genius" (H. 479; Sc. 812). One day man will be awake and asleep at the same time.[2]

Novalis joins to this idea of duality the idea that genius is a plurality, an internal society of different individuals, heterogeneous to one another, who dialogue within one and the same being (B. 37, 428, 445; Sc. 71, 78; H. 529, 662). All true thinking is dialogue and all true sensation is sympathy (Sc. 226). To be a genius is to be in company with oneself. Thus is born a commerce of extremes, of spirituality and sensuality (Sc. 226). The genius is a person to the second power.

This union of contraries is chanted by Novalis in his poem "The Marriage of the Seasons."

Novalis's aesthetics is dominated by this idea of necessary and fecund contradiction. Something is only expressed in its opposite (B. 70). A poetic work will be infinitely poetic and yet simple at the same time (H. 750; Sc. 860: on the union of multiple subjects and simple operations). It contains both resolution and freedom, determinacy and indeterminacy (Sc. 37, 392; H. 641). It manifests a unification of rest and movement, enthusiasm and reason (H. 79), truth that elevates and illusion that resolves (B. 10), the strange and familiar (Sc. 04),[3] clarity and mystery (Sc. 312), order and disorder: through the veil of order we perceive a glimmering chaos (Sc. 375). Poetic meaning is the sense of the necessary-contingent (Sc. 378).

All poetry should be epic, hymn, and drama at once (Sc. 391), tragedy and comedy at once, linked together in a symbolic and unknowable relation (B. 77; H. 824). Beyond mere playfulness and sadness, can be reached a cheerful gravity (77; H. 754). Even further, the arts are united in each other: in every work of art, painting, music, and poetry are present (Sc. 403).

2. An example: nobody more than Novalis has seen that illness refines and spiritualizes, that sorrow intensifies. No one has insisted more that "our original existence is ecstasy and pleasure." If all unhappiness is long and every pleasure short, it is because time emerges with unhappiness whereas pleasure is naturally something that has no relation with time (121).

3. Hence in *Henry of Ofterdingen* the two feelings of *déjà vu* and *jamais vu* ["never seen before"] are constantly following one another and being united.

Thus constituted, art will be finally joined to nature. The genius will make of nature an art and of art a nature.

In the realm of thought, this life of genius described by Novalis will consist of a union of discourse and intuition (H. 277; Sc. 8), of the internal and external. This last idea will lead to a realist idealism in which the two opposed doctrines will be united (Sc. 27). If isolated, idealism and realism are equally errors (H. 840, 912), as Hamann saw. In reality they prove one another. Their antinomy itself is their demonstration. In a general way, it could be shown how antinomy and demonstration are identical. To say that all is demonstrable is to say that all is antinomical. Realism and idealism morph into each other (H. 926, 927). There is hence an "idealization" of realism and a "realization" of idealism (H. 927). But even this thought according to which each leads to the other can be surpassed when one discovers that they coincide (H. 926).

Here we see three modes of thought which help Novalis unite contraries. The first could be termed a dialectical method or, in order to use Novalis's own word, an elastic manner of thinking, which consists in passing from one extreme to the other and back. The sensible ought to be spiritualized, the spiritual sensualized (B. 523); the body ought to become soul and the soul body (B. 373; H. 1057); the serious ought to shine forth in a cheerful way, and joy in a serious way (B. 7; H. 829). What is familiar ought to become strange and the strange familiar: this is the essence of Romanticism. Everything involuntary ought to be transformed into something voluntary, and everything voluntary ought to become something necessary and natural (B. 371, 400).

In some moments, there will occur a kind of coincidence of opposites by passing deeper into one of the extremes. Hence for activity and passivity: "Activity is the faculty of reception" (H. 642). In fact this is an idea to which Novalis attaches great importance. Passivity is not as contemptible as is believed (H. 971), and even the act of enjoyment and of letting things happen appears in fact nobler than the act of accomplishment, of production. Contemplation is nobler than action (B. 166). Absolute passivity is a perfect conductor; absolute activity is a perfect nonconductor. Thus activity ought to lead to passivity. "One does not create, but only does what one can" (B. 299). There is a

moment when all activity ceases (Sc. 282). At a certain level of sensation, one is by oneself, without personal activity, virtuous and genial
(B. 299). The spirit is essential tranquillity (Sc. 282). Being "in a poetic
state," and "in a state of absolute creativity," is at the same time being in
a state of pure passivity.

Finally, in other moments, we are led no longer to a dialectical
movement, to a coincidence of opposites, but to a synthesis. It is here
above all that the thought of Novalis prepares the way for Hegel. We
have already seen the synthesis he wants to achieve between realism
and idealism. His idea of the genius leads to a kind of concrete universal. Sometimes he is startlingly near to the idea: "True poetic characters
are at the same time voices and diverse instruments. They should be
general and particular at the same time" (Sc. 392). Every national, temporal, and local is allowed to universalize, canonize, and generalize.
He speaks of an individual and universal color (B. 233). Romanticism,
he says, is essentially the universalization of the individual moment
(H. 970). The more nature is individual, the more it becomes generally
interesting (Sc. 392). "Union of the general and special. The general
and the special diversify to infinity" (H. 810).

For Novalis, a thing is only proved by its opposite, only expressed
through its opposite. Even more, it must accomplish itself in its opposite. Yet even more, it is itself its union with its opposite.

All of this effort is an attempt to show within the human condition a condition of the suprahuman condition: it ought to be overcome. "The act of leaping beyond oneself is everywhere and always the
highest act, the original point, the genesis of life. The flame is nothing
but an action of this kind. Thus philosophy begins where philosophy
philosophizes about itself, that is, simultaneously, burns up, causes
itself, and is fulfilled" (Sc. 271).

From "Wahl's Famous Lecture"

(Meeting of the Société française de philosophie, December 4, 1937)

INTRODUCTORY NOTE AND *DRAMATIS PERSONAE* OF DECEMBER 4, 1937

by William C. Hackett

These extracts from the discussion and the letters submitted to the meeting of the Société française de philosophie are included as a long appendix to Wahl's original book. They present virtually the entire discussion unchanged: only one oral contribution and one letter that appeared in the *Bulletin* of the society were excised from the book, as my annotations make plain below.

Before the translation of this final part of Wahl's book, I provide a list of participants in the meeting, meant especially to offer orienting remarks about the lesser-known figures.

Aron, Raymond (1905–1983). French political philosopher, sociologist, and journalist; professor at the Sorbonne. Highly influenced by Max Weber, Aron exposed the highly dogmatic nature of modern, secular ideologies, coining the term *secular religion*. He later wrote the famous *Opium of the Intellectuals* (1955) criticizing the blind embrace of Marxism by many thinkers of his day.

Bastide, Georges (1901–1969). Moral philosopher at the University of Toulouse. His thought, concerned in the main with the problem of

93

values, takes its starting point from the conviction that man perpetually desires the good which ever-exceeds him, and that therefore his
life is marked by an unrest that becomes acutely manifest in moral
decision making. This unrest discloses to human consciousness both
the value inherent in things and the correlation of desire with the
Absolute, understood as the origin of all value.

Berdyaev, Nicolai (1874–1948). Russian aristocrat and intellectual
expelled from Russia by the Bolsheviks; author of numerous works of
"Christian existentialism," including *The Freedom of the Spirit* (1927)
and *The Beginning and the End* (1947).

Berthelot, René (1872–1960). Professor of Philosophy at the University of Brussels until 1907; author of influential studies of evolution in
philosophy and pragmatism.

Bespaloff, Rachel (1895–1949). Existentialist philosopher and literary
critic from Bulgaria; emigrated to the United States from France in
1942 to escape persecution of Jews; author of *On the Iliad: A Study of
Homer's Interpretation of Man in War and in Peace* (1947). She sailed
to the United States with Wahl and committed suicide there in 1949.

Brunschvicg, Léon (1869–1944). Professor of Philosophy at the Sorbonne until he fled from the Nazis to Southern France; an influential
interpreter of Descartes, he initiated an important strain of French idealism for which judgment, as the synthesis of thought into concepts, creates
the world of spirit, the only possible world of philosophical inquiry, as he
already set out in his early work *La modalité du jugement* (1897). Brunschvicg cofounded both the influential journal *Revue de Métaphysique et
Morale*, in 1893, and the Société française de philosophie, in 1901.

Delacroix, Henri (1873–1937). Influential psychologist; teacher at
the Sorbonne; author of important books, on the psychology of the
mystics in particular. Delacroix's appearance in the meeting was only
in the memories of those present. He died, according to the minutes
recorded in the *Bulletin*, on the previous afternoon, December 3, 1937.

Brunschvicg, the moderator of the meeting, introduced the meeting with a moving elegy to Delacroix's life and thought. I translate here some extracts from his words:[1] "Bad news circulates quickly. . . . Early yesterday afternoon, Henri Delacroix suddenly died, after a long, unsettling illness, with which, however, he seemed at peace. . . . [This is a moment of] mourning for our society, for philosophy, for the Sorbonne, and for friendship.

"What characterized Henri Delacroix was an extremely acute sensitivity, which impacted others with a profound intimacy: an artistic and religious sensitivity, a living bond with persons in their suffering and in their joy; at the same time, a free and victorious effort to command this sensitivity, in order to justify its value, through an impartial and disinterested attention to the conditions of its objectivity.

"His teaching and books show that nothing escaped him that could sustain and nourish the psychology of art, language, and religion. We know very well our very own meetings where he intervened in order to discuss Saint Thérèse with Émile Boutroux, or Saint John of the Cross with Father Laberthonière and Jean Baruzi. . . . His clear-sightedness in every domain he touched only served to multiply the efficacy of his beneficence. He is not only among those whom we are universally sorry to be without; he is missing and will continue to be missed."

Heidegger, Martin (1889–1976). Heidegger's thought is a central theme of Wahl's presentation, understood in continuity with the "philosophy of existence" deriving from Kierkegaard. Heidegger's brief letter totally rejects Wahl's notion that he himself at least (Jaspers is another question) is engaged in simply a "secularization" of Kierkegaard's religious existentialism. To understand his thought as another existentialism is wholly to misunderstand him.

Hersch, Jeanne (1910–2000). Swiss-Jewish philosopher; a student of Jaspers and the first female professor at the University of Geneva. The main theme of her works is the existentialist conception of freedom.

---

1. [See "Subjectivité et transcendance," *Bulletin de la Société française de philosophie* 37, no. 5 (1937): 163–64.]

Jaspers, Karl (1883–1969). Influential psychiatrist, then philosopher (with a considerable impact on modern theology). Like Heidegger, Jaspers was unsettled by the label "existentialist." He described his own philosophy as *Existenzphilosophie*, which he once defined as "to catch sight of reality at its origin and to grasp it through the way in which I, in thought, deal with myself."[2] Well before 1937, both Heidegger and Jaspers sought to distinguish clearly their philosophies from each other.

Landsberg, Paul (1901–1944). Jewish-Christian existentialist philosopher; a student of Husserl and Heidegger and close associate of Emmanuel Mounier in Paris; author of *The Experience of Death: The Moral Problem of Suicide* (1951). Landsberg died in the concentration camp at Oranienburg.

Lavelle, Louis (1883–1951.) Professor of Philosophy at the Sorbonne; a thinker in the stream of French "spiritualism" (opposed to "materialism") after Bergson. For Lavelle, the domain of metaphysics was the "first-person" domain of subjective experience (opposed to the "third-person" domain of science). A major figure in his day, he is now all but forgotten. Articles on Lavelle and translations into English of selections from his numerous works can be found on the website of the Association Louis Lavelle (http://association-lavelle.chez-alice.fr/).

Lenoir, Raymond (1890–1972). Parisian philosopher and student of Emile Durkheim at the Sorbonne. Lenoir participated in another famous meeting of the Société française de la philosophie (1931), on "la notion de philosophie chrétienne," with Gilson, Maritain, and others.[3]

Levinas, Emmanuel (1906–1995). A close associate of Wahl's; Levinas, in his letter, rejects Wahl's interpretation of continuity between

---

2. [*Philosophy of Existence*, trans. Richard Grabau (Philadelphia: University of Pennsylvania Press, 1971), 3.]

3. [Session of March 31, 1931; published in the society's *Bulletin* 31, no. 2 (1931).]

Heidegger and Kierkegaard, and instead suggests that Wahl's reading does not yet see what is radically at stake with Heideggerian transcendence.

Löwith, Karl (1897–1973). Jewish-Christian philosopher from Munich; a student of Heidegger; fled Germany in 1934; like Wahl and others at this event, he lived and taught in the United States during the 1940s. Löwith is the author of *Meaning in History* (1949), which argues that the modern concept of history has roots in Christian eschatology.

Marcel, Gabriel (1889–1973). Philosopher and playwright. His 1949–50 Gifford Lectures became his famous work *The Mystery of Being* (2 vols.). Similar to Jaspers, Marcel came to reject the term *existentialism* to describe his own thought. In his case this was especially meant to distinguish himself sharply from the crass materialism of existentialists like Sartre. He ultimately preferred the term *neo-Socratism*. A close associate and friend of Wahl, Marcel serves as his main interlocutor in the meeting.

Marck, Siegfried (1889–1957). Jewish neo-Kantian and socialist; student of Heinrich Rickert; taught philosophy at the University of Breslau (where Heidegger would block his appointment to full professor in 1930); subsequently exiled to France and then emigrated to America.

Nadler, Käte. German philosopher influenced particularly by Richard Kroner (of *Von Kant bis Hegel* fame); author of numerous studies on Hegel. Her most influential work was her doctoral dissertation, *Der dialektische Widerspruch in Hegels Philosophie und das Paradoxon des Christentums* (1931) comparing Kierkegaardian (Barthian) "paradox" to Hegelian "contradiction," arguing that Christian paradox finds its highest expression, actually, in Hegel.

Pollnow, Hans (1902–1943). German psychiatrist and translator of philosophical works; fled Nazi-German persecution by emigrating to France in 1933. Pollnow was captured during the Occupation and died in the concentration camp at Mauthausen.

Rougemont, Denis de (1906–1985). Swiss philosopher who lived in Paris; author of *Love in the Western World* (1939/1972), which explores the Western conception of love as the union and conflict of passion and commitment.

Wahl, Jean (1888–1974). Wahl was a last-minute replacement for this meeting. As Brunschvicg notes in his opening remarks, the original speaker was a certain "Monsieur Leroux," whose wife's sudden illness forced him to withdraw.[4]

DISCUSSION

The paper "Subjectivity and Transcendence" was presented at a meeting of the Société française de philosophie on December 4, 1937. I present here some extracts from the discussion that followed as well as from some of the letters submitted to the author on this occasion.[5]

GABRIEL MARCEL: We read in the text provided for us: "We could ask if 'transascendence' is necessarily good, and 'transdescendence'

---

4. [See the *Bulletin* (1937): 164.]

5. [Léon Brunschvicg, who moderated the meeting, inaugurated the discussion in this way: "I believe that Monsieur Gabriel Marcel, who has known Wahl's thought as long as Wahl has known it, would like to be the first to respond?" (172). Marcel then began his live remarks with: "My intervention will bear on the written text rather than on Wahl's oral presentation, because the latter seems to me to be attenuated in comparison to what we have read, especially on the point that occupies me most. I will not try, moreover, to interpret this divergence, which seems very sensible to me.

"Obviously the first part of the presentation will not be the focus of my remarks. When it comes to Kierkegaard, I am extremely less competent. I have the impression, by the way, that everything that has been said is true and concerns an essential element of Kierkegaardian thought. By contrast, I feel myself to be much less in agreement with the remarks presented thereafter" (173).]

necessarily bad."[6] Let us admit, even though this is probably not actually the case, that the meaning of these two terms *transascendence* and *transdescendence* is made sufficiently precise by the references which follow them: Blake, Gide, . . . et alia. But what remain in any case completely vague are the words *good* and *bad*. And I think for at least several of the poets invoked—I will say in any case in Lawrence and Cowper Powys, and very probably also in Gide—provided that we consider the entire scope of his thought—the same thing can be said: the idea of good and evil has not been submitted to a rigorous enough reflection. We must begin, then, by explaining the meaning of these two words as they appear in the sentence I just quoted.

I'm guessing the good is that which exalts our powers, or our feeling of this power? From this point of view it is in fact tempting to say that transdescendence could be good. In other words, in more precise language, at least more understandable, that in putting a very strong accent on the subterranean parts of ourselves, or, if you like, on the dark God—it is not difficult to find, in Lawrence in particular, some analogous expressions—one would be intensifying within us a certain immediate awareness of our existence conceived as force.

I would say that this is not a discovery, not even a paradox, but a truism. I wish to emphasize that this affirmation only has meaning if we begin by denaturing the idea of the good, that is, by accepting a bioenergetic meaning. On the contrary, the more we retain a preoccupation with remaining in agreement with the great spiritual tradition of humanity—it is not a matter here of Occidentalism—the more this affirmation appears devoid of meaning. But I wonder if we will not refuse carefully enough to explain as I have just done this radical change of meaning to the words *good* and *evil* if we do not somehow take our chances with the uncertainty that we find there.

In a general way, I would say that in speaking of transdescendence in opposition to transascendence we are merely, it seems to me,

6. [Marcel refers to the text that composes the first part of the chapter "Subjectivity and Transcendence," above, which was provided for the members of the Société française de philosophie in anticipation of their meeting, featuring Wahl's presentation of the same name.]

recalling what Schelling perfectly understood after Boehme: that the order of powers is reversible, and as far as I am concerned every philosophy that fails to recognize this possibility is in a sense completely obsolete. Only let me immediately add that philosophy is required to take a position in the face of this reversal, of taking it directly for what it is, that is, as a subversion, and it is precisely this that Schelling in particular never failed to do.

I think that if philosophy abstains from taking sides in that way in the presence of this reversal, it risks *selling out*. If treason is possible in philosophy, this is it. And this is exactly what, I would say, all the kinds of thinking that make a pact with an infrarational element are guilty of. And this is the point where I think that an agreement is made with the greatest ease between the philosophies of existence as I conceive them and a certain rationalism. Here I suppose that what should be addressed is the Nietzschean idea of transvaluation, *Umwertung*, and its implicit confusion of a will toward purification, a militant sincerity always more attentive to its own exigencies (which is the essential component of Nietzsche's thought, and a sort of will toward subversion of fundamental values that takes root either in a collection of complex disquisitions as postulates, or in a naturalist metaphysics).

I will not easily accept the remark that transcendence is not necessarily God or the devil, but perhaps simply nature. Here again it seems to me that a certain conceptual imprecision can be traced back to an uncertainty in the thinker's purposes. What does it mean to say "transcendence can be simply nature"? With nature being opposed to God, it seems that your observation can be reduced to: "nature can be itself experienced as being beyond the conceivable according to certain norms." All the great lyrics almost without exception testify to this experience. It is simply a given. The philosophical problem is posed from this word, from this nature naturing and not nature natured. It is only here opposed to God because one is given, although again without explanation, a certain idea of God, for example as moral order of the world if you like, or perhaps as person, and so forth.

The question remains if, at the heart of this nature naturing, there is not to be distinguished, to be opposed, as the Romantics believed, a hierarchy of powers, the order of which can be, once again, reversed.

These remarks call for the response that I will make as far as the questions of the last paragraph concern me: can we conceive of a philosophy like Heidegger and Jaspers's, the attraction of which is not partly explained by the fact that it consists of a nostalgia and echo of the religious? I would not speak here of an "attraction." Instead, the problem is a matter of knowing if a philosophy of existence can be conceived without reference to the transcendent. Apparently, or if we are concerned only with the formal aspect of ideas, it certainly can. But the question still remains whether an existence not related to an inexhaustible transcendent does not just degenerate into pure facticity. Is it not the case that this philosophy of existence would be reduced to a schematic of observation? The danger of linking the philosophy of existence too directly to theology was pointed out. What does this mean? I detect here a peril that is real indeed: that the philosopher causes to crop up not elements of theology, but of an overly determined theology, and by that betrays [the cause of philosophy itself].

Here again a very careful examination is required. The idea of sin or fall as it appears in existential philosophy—does it not translate a fundamental given handed over to reflection as soon as we become fully aware of the situation that composes our existence? This is how I understand Jaspers, and even Heidegger.

It is a matter of seeing the intrinsic worth of these analyses. If they are found to coincide to some degree with the assertions of theology, it does not automatically mean we should be induced to defiance—if these analyses are accepted as accurate. Especially because, after all, we ought to wonder where these theological ideas came from. They did not fall from heaven.

Finally, a word on why I cannot go all the way with the final remark. The existence of Rimbaud, Nietzsche, or Hölderlin is not in itself philosophical or existential. You present these figures, however ambiguously, merely as functions of a philosophy of existence. What will prevent me, if I am a doctor, from treating the fate of Nietzsche as a clinical case, that is, syphilographically? Objectively nothing, absolutely nothing. One is always completely free to be totally baffled. But then it is a matter of justifying this other point of view, this existential viewpoint. This is philosophy, and it alone can do this—by showing that on a certain level (though it is necessary to establish it on this level) the pathological particularities that are unique to Nietzsche are void of meaning or at the very least possess a signification that should be interpreted based on a whole.

The conclusion of this set of remarks is, first, that what is given here does not add up to a philosophy. I think that it is completely vain to claim so. After all, the philosophies of existence are perhaps much less important than the lives that do the existing. What is doubtlessly true is that these lives are essential, and I even think—I will go so far as to say—that a philosophy of existence can likely be constituted *in concreto* only as "monography" (I do not like this word), or in other words through references to lives blessed with a certain tragic signification. Nothing seems to me to be more correct.

This does not mean, once again, that the consideration of these privileged lives is somehow sufficient in itself. I do not even see how one could think that.

Finally—and this is the point that I take most personally to heart, and on which a discussion could usefully ensue—I do not believe for a minute that a philosophy, existential if you like, can take any liberty with fundamental values. More precisely, it is doubtlessly capable of doing that, to the degree that, as philosophy, it is, if you like, freedom in action. It only remains to be seen whether this freedom, exercised in this way, I will say in a self-destructive fashion, is not its own annihilation.

JEAN WAHL: It is certainly the case, when I spoke of "transascendence" and "transdescendence," that I have tied down the word *transdescendence*, attaching it to what Kierkegaard said, and hence with the idea of demonic force, and from that moment it takes on a moral dimension, and even an immoral dimension. I wanted to remain outside of these categories of the moral and immoral. I wanted to say—as in fact you said—that there are ways to reach the deep forces of being, and that this transdescendence is not degeneration. I did not want to say that evil is good. That is a problem with which I am not presently concerned. Have I betrayed [philosophy] by saying what I said? I do not believe so. But I believe that many betray philosophy who want to intervene with questions of morality and value when the question is really a matter of pure knowledge.

Here it is not a matter of saying what is good or evil, and I was wrong in this sense to employ those words. It is instead a matter of remaining in the realm of a kind of contemplation, whether it be sensory or artistic or metaphysical, of finding what in fact increases our knowledge and intensifies our spontaneity.

Your second objection pertains to the idea of nature. You say that nature is here divinized. It is possible. But it depends. Do you think the idea of divinization strictly entails the idea of a God? I mean: do you think that there is not actually a more primitive idea somewhere in there? I am trying precisely to return to this something more primitive. For a number of reasons the word *nature* is perhaps not very well chosen. I think I originally said "the world" and "the external world"— words equally insufficient. There is no word. I want to speak of the other that is neither necessarily the God of the religions, nor even of their heterodoxies.

You said that there cannot be philosophical reflection without transcendence. But I am struck by the fact that in Spencer, for example, there is transcendence, but we cannot find in him—I cannot find it in any case—this tension that I investigate in Kierkegaard. This does not depend on whether or not there is transcendence; what it also depends on is one's attitude toward things. A philosopher with transcendence like Spencer is not very satisfying. And there can be this philosopher or that artist without transcendence who, by his intensity, gives me much more the impression of summoning up from within myself something from the depths.

As for the feeling of fallenness, I am not sure if we have it or not. It is a question for reflection. Do we primordially possess the feeling of the original fall? Sometimes we have a feeling of solitude, we have a feeling of angst, if you like, but I do not know if we naturally possess the feeling of fallenness.

For the artists and philosophers I mentioned at the end of my paper, I think a distinction should be made, for example, between Nietzsche and Rimbaud or Van Gogh, and then a distinction would have to be made between Rimbaud and Van Gogh. But there is surely a philosophical reflection in Nietzsche, and even in Rimbaud, and even, further, in Van Gogh, if we refer to some of his letters. So I do not see why I should be prohibited from turning toward them as philosophical sources. For this is precisely the way that I turn toward them. You say that, by themselves, they cannot be interpretations and responses. But that does not seem evident to me. You also say that Nietzsche could be explained by psychoanalysis. But perhaps inasmuch as Heidegger's philosophy touches the depths of being, it could also be explained by psychoanalysis.

GABRIEL MARCEL: I would like to respond point by point.

First, it seems to me to be essential to analyze the idea of depth. For I think that here we have some dreadful equivocations. The elemental is, in one sense, the profound. But in another sense, it is not at all the profound. In reality, we should use these flattened-out metaphors prudentially. With them we cannot be more careful, I think.

In relation to my first objection, you spoke of pure knowledge. But we do not inhabit the order of knowledge; we are always in the order of evaluation. You say that the words *good* and *evil* with their moral resonance are perhaps not required here. All the same, it is necessary to substitute others, which are also themselves terms that express a judgment of value. Consequently, if we are in the realm of judgment (and it seems to me that if we are not there, then we are nowhere, for if it is not a matter of explanation, we are absolutely not involved with explanatory theory), if you introduce an evaluation, I believe that my objection reappears.

Moving to the second point, the transcendence of nature. You said: "I am not sure that nature, such as, for example, it is given in the great lyrics, is divinized. Is the idea of God truly found there?" I am terribly wary of the word *idea*. Certainly, if we place ourselves on an ideological terrain, we could quickly find ourselves in agreement with everything you are looking for. But what is important here is attitude. It is difficult to deny that in Schelling, for example, there is a certain attitude of adoration before nature. This is sufficient for me to speak of a sort of diffuse theology. It seems to me that you are using the words *God* and *theology* in a determined, hyper-Christian sense. But there could be a non-Christian theology. Really, it is this which is critical here.

It is not a matter of words. The term you use here is very important. Is it the case that, as soon as the term *transcendence* is introduced, to some degree one is doing theology? I do not think that the idea of transcendence, stretched to the limit, is secularizable. This is the expression I would use.

The third point. Regarding existence, you evoke Spencer. This is a man who has perhaps never reflected, and who, at the very least, probably has no idea about what we are able to call transcendence. I will therefore not speak about transcendence in relation to his doctrine. Here we are playing with analogies that are purely verbal. You cannot say that transcendence in Kierkegaard or Heidegger has anything in common with Spencer's unknown—perhaps precisely because Spencer always inhabits a realm of knowledge. He is an intellectualist to the tenth degree, but he is all the same an intellectualist. He has not at all risen to a superior realm. Everything you said at the beginning on the relations of objectivity and transcendence, which is important and ought to be elaborated, is in contradiction with everything we find in Spencer. So I will not accept your use of Spencer as an example. With him, it seems to me, the problem is not even posed. We are not in the subjective, but in the infraobjective.

Regarding the feeling of fallenness: this remains a question that appears to me to be very ambiguous. It seems like you are asking this question for the sake of a potential investigation. Could it be said that all being finds in itself, in some way, this feeling or experience? I would say that it is infinitely likely that no, in any case, there is not this awareness. But I do not care at all about this; it does not interest me, and I would be the first to recognize that a sole being, a single soul where we truly find this experience or feeling to a certain degree of intensity and clarity, counts much more than millions who in short have no interior life at all.

On the other hand, it is difficult for me to subscribe to what you say about Nietzsche, Rimbaud, Van Gogh, et alia. First because I think that this *rapprochement* is altogether fallacious. Nietzsche is all the same a philosopher. That distorts everything. The problem that you pose exists in pure form only if you take artists who are in no way philosophers. From this point of view, if you wish to take it, Van Gogh, and I would say the same about Rimbaud, are more satisfying examples. But the question of interpretation remains. How can you make out of it an abstraction? Do they themselves furnish us with all the elements of this interpretation? This is not certain. We are here required to pose a methodological problem. When you say, at the end, after all, the philosophy of Heidegger itself can be considered in a certain way as a phenomenon subject to psychoanalysis like the experience of Rimbaud, you are not taking into account the difference between this philosophy and a nonphilosophy: above all, this philosophy is an effort to explain its own postulates. To the degree that Heidegger's philosophy contains psychoanalytic elements, supposing that this is the case, it will admit this. And for me it is philosophy only on this condition. This is why I am always obliged to use this term, *explication*. This is the entire question. Starting from the point where there is explication, there is philosophy, and starting from there alone.

You say that lives like that are philosophical lives. I agree. I do not see any problem there. Only, are these sources of philosophy, somehow independently from the philosophers who interpret them and comment on them? It seems to me sufficient to pose this question in order then to resolve it.

JEAN WAHL: I think you risk diminishing philosophy, whereas I want to exalt it by saying that it exists as much in "nonphilosophers as in philosophers." I do not see that philosophy should simply be defined as explication. When its postulates are implicit, then it is not philosophy? No. I would say that precisely in Rimbaud, whose postulates I am not entirely familiar with, there is not philosophy, but a source of philosophy. In this case you would say that I am in agreement with you since you admit that in Rimbaud there is a source of philosophy? The difference being that, according to you, the philosopher is the one who will reflect upon what is in another in an existential state?

GABRIEL MARCEL: Not necessarily. For I think that without a doubt the greatest are those who have been at once their own poet and their own philosopher. When you say that I am making philosophy a function of pure explication, you are deforming somewhat my thought. I believe that there is truly philosophy only where there is a certain interior creation that is absolutely fundamental. What I am saying is that if this creation is not accompanied by a reflection on itself, it is prephilosophical or periphilosophical. Here the example of Kierkegaard is significant.

JEAN WAHL: It is no less significant in the sense that he is an example of both. He is the model of a life that is not completely explicit . . . He is the model of someone who I can put on the same level as Nietzsche and even Rimbaud and Van Gogh, upon whom you doubtlessly bestow the name philosopher.

GABRIEL MARCEL: A failed philosophy.

JEAN WAHL: It is rather the source of philosophy, but a source that seems to me to be at least as great as philosophy.

GABRIEL MARCEL: As great . . . We are not asking the question in these terms. Who would dream of establishing a comparison between the grandeur of an artist and a philosopher? I do not see any meaning at all to this question. What I simply want to say is that a certain creation not accompanied by reflection is incomplete, is a creation that needs the other, and which is extended toward the other, even though, despite all, for me, if we remain faithful to a certain traditional idea, the philosopher is all the same *autarkes*.

JEAN WAHL: The essence of man is precisely that in him nothing is accomplished that is not at the same time reflection on that which he accomplishes, starting, at least, from a certain level. In Van Gogh or Rimbaud you cannot say that there is no reflection on what happens in them. So then, for you it would be a matter of completely putting philosophical reflections to one side, and to the other side a reflection that is not philosophical?

GABRIEL MARCEL: Rimbaud's case is very depressing. When we look at the absolutely contradictory interpretations that continue to be proposed through Rimbaud's evolution, we are forced to conclude that there is not found in Rimbaud himself anything to help shed light on him. I am not saying that this observation diminishes him at all, but it does not allow us to make him a philosopher.

JEAN WAHL: A great philosopher—and this is what in part composes his value—cannot be completely illumined.

GABRIEL MARCEL: I share this opinion with you. It is even certain that to the degree that a philosopher is inserted into a history, he calls out for interpretations that come after him. But we still have to say that all the same he has made a certain effort of self-interpretation. This does not mean that this self-interpretation is sufficient.

JEAN WAHL: This seems very difficult to me. I well see that Rimbaud does not express himself in the academic-speak that we use here, and that Heidegger more approaches the philosophical classroom. But I do not see at all that there is any less profound reflection in Rimbaud than in Heidegger. We would have to study the mode of reflection that you are calling philosophy.

GABRIEL MARCEL: At the risk of scandalizing all the disciples of Rimbaud, I would say that the greater the artist, the more he is reduced to a phenomenon; to the degree that there is the Rimbaud-phenomenon, what you say applies to him, but on the condition of refusing for him this *autarkeia*, the act of holding within oneself one's own interpretation.

LÉON BRUNSCHVICG: Perhaps there are some autarkic philosophers who would like to intervene in order to arbitrate the debate?

RENÉ BERTHELOT: I would translate your two philosophical terms—*subjectivity* and *transcendence*—by two others that are to a large degree aesthetic and religious and which seem to me to indicate better who Kierkegaard was. In his thought subjectivity is Romanticism and transcendence is Calvinism. And if I were to try to define him by a formula that is fatally incomplete (like every formula of this kind), I would say that he was a Romantic Calvinist, and that is how he is distinguished both from other Romantics and other Calvinists.

In the first place, Kierkegaard (1813–55) seems to me functionally a Romantic, and, to be more precise, a German Romantic. He made a good claim that, his religious faith allowing him—so he says—to overcome subjectivity, he is thereby opposed to Romanticism, though we nevertheless find in him all the dominant traits. This is what Georg Brandès demonstrated in his study on German Romanticism, numerous chapters of which cite or summarize Kierkegaard in order to show point by point that his thought and his literary conception approach either that of Tieck (with his belief in the metaphysical meaning of music and humor), or that of Novalis, or of the Schlegel brothers, et alia. Brandès being Danish like Kierkegaard, and the influence of Kierkegaard being very great in the Denmark of Brandès's time, it is natural that he wanted to show to his countrymen that Kierkegaard was not an isolated phenomenon, an aerolite, but rather a Danish reflection of the sensibilities, literary forms, and philosophical thought of the German Romantics.

Therefore I think that if one takes him in his concrete individuality and historicity, it is indispensable to begin by returning him to this current of German Romanticism.

JEAN WAHL: What I wanted to do is to separate him from this current in order to take him as he is in himself.

RENÉ BERTHELOT: But do you not risk deforming his physiognomy by isolating him, abstracting him from this current, if it is the case that taking him in himself and in his concrete reality are inseparable? If I insist on this point, it is because the thought of Kierkegaard does not seem to me to have a contemporary impact to the degree that German Romanticism has preserved one. What do we encounter in Kierkegaard? Precisely what we encounter with much more richness, creative poetic power, and philosophical depth in the great German Romantics. In some respects, Kierkegaard's thought is tied to Schelling's reaction, in his old age, to Hegel. But to take him more broadly, his subjectivism corresponds to an attitude intermediary between Fichte and Schelling. One recognizes in him something of the second Fichte and the first Schelling, during the period when these two were most directly related. Here is found a form of philosophical Romanticism that lasted only a few years, and the thought of Kierkegaard as a theory of subjectivity is linked—not exclusively but especially—to this era of German thought.

I pass to the second point: transcendence. As I said, I think that for us to approach Kierkegaard in his concrete individuality and historical reality we should set him squarely within the Calvinist current. He is conceived as isolated not only from other men, but from God. This shows up in his violent attacks on the official Danish church. And this double isolation, as you have said, is essential for him.

But we recognize this in Ibsen's character Brand,[7] and we know from Georg Brandès that this tragic figure was inspired by the personality of Kierkegaard. He portrays very well the double mark of transcendence in Kierkegaard, isolation in relation to his relatives, and the fact of conceiving his God as unattainable.

In certain of Ibsen's heroes, as in Ibsen himself, there is what could be called a Calvinism without Christianity. Huxley (the elder, the friend of Darwin) said of Auguste Comte that his philosophy was a Catholicism without Christianity. There has even been for a half century now a certain number of thinkers and writers who one could say come from a Protestantism without Christianity, and for many of their number, a Calvinism without Christianity. This Calvinist pessimism ceaselessly marked Ibsen's theatrical legacy to the end. Jean-Gabriel Borkman[8] still resembles Brand. And in the playwright a durable influence of Kierkegaard's thought remains, in the sense that you have defined it through the word *transcendence*. At the time that he sought to separate himself from the Romanticism of his youth and to break from traditional Protestantism, a persistence of the moral attitude of Calvinism remained. And, by virtue of the more literary than philosophical nature of the Kierkegaardian spirit, it is without a doubt in a playwright like Ibsen rather than among the philosophers that

7. [Brand was the main character in Ibsen's 1865 play of the same name.]
8. [The main character of Ibsen's 1896 play of the same name.]

we ought to look for his most authentic heir. Kierkegaard is situated between Calvin and Ibsen.

In this way could be discerned those among his contemporaries to whom the Danish writer appears to be the closest, in sentiment, thought or literary manner. It is to Carlyle that we look, the Carlyle above all of the first period. The solitary Scotsman from Craigenputtock was of Puritan (hence Calvinist) formation as well as of Romantic forma- tion (as defined by German Romanticism, from which he received his "unarticulated" "song" and his tormented sense of humor, so close to Kierkegaard's own). Kierkegaard is a sort of Danish Carlyle who would have remained *Sartor resartus*, who would not have been subjected to the influence of Saint-Simonism, and dedicated to historical research.

From that I equally believe that we can draw some general conclu- sions about the use certain philosophers today make of Kierkegaard.

Can some of the central themes of his thought be made the point of departure for a philosophical doctrine? This is the problem that you have asked.

I will not go into the thought of Heidegger and Jaspers in any detail. Let a general indication be sufficient: it seems to me that these very dif- ferent philosophies offer us above all the reflection bouncing off of a very particular state of the soul, and it is therefore quixotic to claim to interpret this state of soul as justified in its totality by a metaphysical doctrine that aims for universality. The mostly aesthetic character of Kierkegaard's thought is one of the reasons that makes it difficult and, in my opinion, illegitimate to interpret as belonging to the same genre. And this critique seems to me to redound in many respects onto the Kierkegaardians about whom you have spoken, despite all the differ- ences that separate these philosophers from their master. On this point I also do not find myself in disagreement with you.

I turn back to Schelling, from whom in philosophy Kierkegaard takes inspiration. For Schelling furnishes us with the elements by which we can compose a judgment not only of Kierkegaard but also of the Kierkegaardians of our day.

In an early work, *The System of Transcendental Idealism*, Schell- ing declared, profoundly, that what is both necessary and incompre- hensible in the development of spirit is the passage from "primitive limitation" to "derivative limitation." Grossly speaking, primitive limitation is the necessity for spirit to manifest itself as a finite and individual ego. Derivative limitation is its act of being precisely this finite ego, precisely this individual ego that I am, in this instant of time, and no such other ego different from the one in such another instant. But, following Schelling, from the moment that spirit poses in the ego primitive limitation, it is impossible for it not to pose by the very same spiritual act derivative limitation. But, on the other hand, derivative limitation, the very particularity that I myself am, cannot escape from primitive limitation. What is simultaneously necessary and incomprehensible in philosophy, says Schelling, is therefore this passage from primitive to derived limitation. But wanting to interpret through a metaphysics that has a universal value—either Kierkegaard or the particular psychological cases analyzed by Heidegger and Jaspers, to which they pretended to attribute a universal value—is for the philosopher precisely to attempt this illegitimate, incomprehensible passage from primitive to derived limitation. And in this way, Schelling's formula seems to me implicitly to contain the critique both of the general attitude of Kierkegaard and the contemporary philosophies you have discussed.

JEAN WAHL: Thank you very much indeed for the views that you have expressed about the elements that formed Kierkegaard's thought.

NICOLAI BERDYAEV: I will offer two remarks.

We should make a distinction between existential philosophy and the philosophy of existence. I believe, fundamentally, that you have created this distinction. For example, Kierkegaard and Nietzsche are existential philosophers. Heidegger and Jaspers are not. Theirs is a philosophy of existence. Existential philosophy is the expression of an existential experience, and it ascribes great value to philosophers themselves as living beings. The philosophy of existence, even if Jaspers says existence can never become an object, makes of existence an object of the philosopher's knowledge.

Another remark. I think there is a great difference between transcendence and the simple supposition that there is a reality above us, an absolute reality, God, the "world beyond." Because transcendence is an existential experience, it is a movement. One could suppose that a world beyond exists. For example Spencer supposes that there is the "unknowable," and at the same time there is no transcendence in the very experience of Spencer and in his philosophy. Nothing happens here, whenever he says, "there is the unknowable"—absolutely nothing. This is exactly the contrary of transcendence as existential experience.

The philosopher, in his knowledge, is able to pass from subjectivity toward the objective, by objectification. And he can pass from subjectivity toward the transcendent by transcendence. These are completely different paths. I think that philosophy becomes less and less existential when the philosopher passes from subjectivity toward objectivity. It remains existential if the philosopher passes from subjectivity toward transcendence. Transcendence is never an object, never an objective world. It is something totally other. When transcendence is turned into an objective world, the exact contrary of an existential philosophy is created. I think the danger in Heidegger and Jaspers is found here—it is not very clear what they are doing: are they moving toward objectivity or transcendence?

In Kierkegaard everything is different.

One cannot remain in subjectivity (not only the philosopher but man himself). But man is a being that exceeds himself, transcends himself. There are different paths that open here, in this passing beyond oneself. Basically Jaspers (in his little book *Vernunft und Existenz*, and others) avers that existential philosophy is not possible. He says this. I think the real interesting thing in the philosophies of Heidegger and Jaspers is that here we have philosophers wounded by the existential experience of Kierkegaard and Nietzsche. Jaspers says this. This experience of Kierkegaard and Nietzsche influenced their philosophy. But even so theirs is not existential philosophy. It would perhaps be paradoxical to say it, but, for example, if we take the philosophy of Hegel, which is totally contrary to the philosophy of Kierkegaard and to existential philosophy as Kierkegaard understood it, it is still more existential than the philosophy of Heidegger or Jaspers because Hegel lived in the dialectic. He experienced it; for him it was existence in a certain sense; an existence totally different from the experience of transcendence, which is a catastrophic experience—and not a development, not an evolution. Hegel inhabited an existence of a completely different kind. But it was all the same a lived philosophy.

JEAN WAHL: I believe I am in complete agreement with you, though the question is open whether Heidegger lives his philosophy. But we do not have the right . . .

NICOLAI BERDYAEV: Every significant philosopher, every true philosopher does so, not only Heidegger. But if we say this, we should say more generally that the only philosophy is existential philosophy, but there is all the same here a certain difference.

PAUL LANDSBERG: I do not want to revisit the problem of existential philosophy, nor speak of Heidegger and Jaspers, because I think Berdyaev has expressed here and in his books manifest verities on this transformation of an existential philosophy into a false objectification of existence. It seems to me that this has irrefutably happened and that it is a tragic and fascinating fall of the mind that occurred there. I want to return to the captivating exchange between Messieurs Wahl and Marcel, particularly on the red-hot point of the problem of—I believe you said—"transascendence" and "transdescendence." In any case, I think I understand what you mean by these terms.

I wonder if perhaps the problem generated by this exchange has not been posed in a sufficiently clear way, and if actually Messieurs Wahl, Marcel, and the rest of us still have some work to do in order first to clarify what the problem actually is. For I think that what we have here is definitely a real problem that exists in itself. If I rightly understand the train of Wahl's thought, he begins—not only in his paper, . . . for I allow myself to speak a little about the history of his thought—he begins from the interpretation of Kierkegaard, finding there a certain description of a lived experience, an existential experience of transcendence.

And it is here that I should say that, for me, what is primary in Kierkegaard is that he is a Christian. He is a believer, a Christian, and all his philosophy, if it is a philosophy, is an interpretation and pedagogy of Christianity, an effort to lead people to a certain realization, to Christianity, to become a serious Christian—it being well understood that *to be* a Christian has no live meaning unless it means always *becoming* Christian. If we abstract from that I think Kierkegaard becomes completely obscure and we can no longer understand him. He is neither a universal philosopher in the sense that Hegel is, nor a Romantic. I do not want to deny what he has in common with German Romanticism, but he is not defined by that Romantic quality—the Christian quality in him is much more serious. I believe Monsieur Wahl and I agree on this point. The transcendence lived by Kierkegaard under a very particular form that you have finely distinguished is Christian transcendence and in any case *a* lived Christian transcendence. Kierkegaard's importance is above all that in his day, in the middle of the nineteenth century, someone lived authentically Christian transcendence and expressed it in a way that belongs to no church, to no theology, but expressed it in a forthrightly dialectical way, in other words in the language of his century, and with all the richness of expression given by Romanticism, poetry, et cetera. You all know that this corresponds closely to Kierkegaard's own interpretation of his vocation: to be a simple Christian who makes use of all the seductions of the language and thought of his century in order to make reunderstood so to speak the Christian situation and faith.

Monsieur Wahl has interpreted the thought of Kierkegaard— and you all know with what profundity he has done so. And he has drawn from it, as Jaspers and Heidegger have done in a completely different way, a certain idea of transcendence as such, which one could yet distinguish from lived Christian experience but which is so to speak this experience in a formalized state. I do not know if the expression is absolutely precise . . . That is, what is of concern here is a transcendence that, indeed, is essentially ascending and finds the *other* in the sacrifice of the *self* and also in the sacrifice of everything natural, of the natural temptation in relation to the self. Kierkegaard, in short, relinquishes the world and his self as a Christian, in order to give himself to his faith, in order to give himself to an ascending transcendence.

Following the train of his thinking, it seems to me that Monsieur Wahl has found that this lived experience that he has seen under a certain form in Kierkegaard has a much more universal meaning, that is, there are other experiences that share some remarkable features with this experience: above all the feature of the experience of the *other* in the strict and absolute sense that Monsieur Wahl has given to it in his interpretation of Kierkegaard. In other words, even in the sphere of biology, of biology as subject of a metaphysics of life, there are ecstasies in which a depersonalizing life takes this character of something absolutely other, in which the self feels the anguish of being lost and to which man, the self, can be given over. In fact, the self is found between two forces . . . that transcend it in this sense. It is true that the self can experience quakes of anguish, feelings analogous to the approach of these two forces, from below and from above, to utilize images, or in any case an essentially spiritual force and an essentially vital force. I believe that the most fecund interpretation would be to speak, after Nietzsche, of Dionysos. In fact, when he says that Dionysos is a god, he means that here it is a matter of a transcendence, that is, that the self is also anguished, sacrificed, destroyed, transcended in being united to Dionysos as in drawing near to a spiritual God. Up to this point I think that from this purely descriptive vantage there is truly an analogy, and up to this point I think that everything that Monsieur Wahl has said is justifiable as is a vantage situated finally closer to Monsieur Marcel. The problem touched on by Monsieur Marcel comes afterward and is a problem not of the philosophy of existence but of existential philosophy, to use the terms introduced by Berdyaev, and therefore that in existential philosophy man exists concretely between these two forces. The self is truly affected by these different forces, and it may grasp the difference between them. Whereas in existential philosophy, though I almost hate to say it—but allow me to in order to express myself with brevity—one attempts to follow a path closer to Kierkegaard, a path taken by men like him, where one can even recognize that there is a collision, not only between the self and an ascending transcendence, but also, after Jean Wahl, between the self and a different transcendence. If the problem of transcendence was only between the self and a sole transcendent "center," things would be much simpler. What you have brought to our attention is much more complex, both that the self is found situated between two forces that oppose it and oppose each other.

From another point of view, where one is already engaged in definite existential philosophy, one could speak with Monsieur Marcel of a "subversion," when a man is given over to a dark ecstasy. Monsieur Marcel has already decided for a certain direction of existence, whereas the point of view of Monsieur Wahl is purely descriptive, and perhaps with a certain penchant for what he calls transdescendence.

JEAN WAHL: I truly have nothing to say but thank you to Monsieur Landsberg.[9]

I would like to extend my thanks to Monsieur Berdyaev by commenting on something he said. I heartily agree in fact that the concept of transcendence greatly needs to be analyzed more deeply than what I was able to do here. To that end we would do well to recall a remark once made by Nicolai Hartmann, who said that we ought not to speak about transcendence but rather of a "movement of what transcends itself toward that which transcends it." This would begin to clarify the discussion. There are movements of transcendence, movements of

9. [In the original meeting there followed here a brief, idiosyncratic remark from Siegfried Marck, which I summarize, I think fairly, in the following way: The entire discussion can be understood as a fundamental critique of the philosophies of existence, and all the points of interrogation "are converging" toward a fundamental solution, namely, in the "absolute dialectic," and a pure "return to immanence," from which they take their point of departure and toward which they inevitably tend. Therefore [?] philosophy will possess a "Platonic" conception of transcendence. Jaspers and Heidegger fail as philosophers inasmuch as they wed the philosophers Kant and Husserl (respectively) to Kierkegaard's nonphilosophy. This contribution was followed by a caustically brief response from Wahl. I quote: "Monsieur Marck says that he agrees with me. I fear that I cannot agree with him regarding the severe judgment he visits on Heidegger and Jaspers. I have much admiration for both of them. Doubtlessly, one of the points of departure for their thought is Kierkegaard, but I think that both possess a very profound elaboration in their own right and a very distinctive tone" (192). Wahl's summative response to the entire discussion which directly followed is included in the book here without change.]

excess. But transcendence should not be applied to the end [*terme*] toward which this movement is directed. Such is Hartmann's observation that perhaps should be contemplated.[10]

Monsieur Berdyaev envisages the same problem that Monsieur Landsberg has very profoundly highlighted: can there be a kind of transcendence toward that which is not the ordinary object of transcendence, toward the object of the movement of transcendence? This is what Monsieur Berdyaev has criticized, and it is this, if I understand him, that Monsieur Landsberg declares possible. But I do not want to end by presenting a solution because I think that the essence of existential philosophy is to tell us that questions have a value in themselves. Philosophical problems cannot be completely resolved. One has to . . . as Rimbaud said . . . make oneself a seer.[11] One has to make oneself the question. And this is why I will not respond.

LETTERS

Translated by Jeffrey Hanson

[As in the original text, the response of Jean Wahl is in italics following each letter.]

10. [The following footnote was added in the book:] Likewise, for Heidegger, the transcendent is not that toward which *Dasein* transcends, but *Dasein* itself. Perhaps immanence and transcendence could be distinguished depending on whether they are found in the theory of reality or the theory of knowledge. In this way Heidegger's philosophy is a philosophy of immanence if seen from the point of view of the theory of reality; it is a theory of transcendence if seen from the point of view of the theory of knowledge. Brunschvicg's theory would be a theory of immanence from the point of view of the theory of knowledge (apart, however, from the "shock") and a theory of transcendence from the point of view of the theory of reality, at least in one sense. Thomism is a theory of transcendence from both perspectives.

But some reservations would have to be stated about these two terms inasmuch as they both preserve a certain echo of their spatial origin.

11. [*Il faut se faire voyant*. From the "Letter to Paul Demeny" (May 15, 1871), from the so-called Visionary Letters.]

Letter from Martin Heidegger

I want to thank you kindly for your friendly invitation to your meeting; unfortunately I am not able to attend because of the current semester's work.

Your critical remarks on the subject of the "philosophy of existence" are very instructive. I should, however, repeat that my philosophical tendencies, although there is a question in *Sein und Zeit* of "*Existenz*" and of "Kierkegaard," are not able to be classed as *Existenzphilosophie*. But this error of interpretation would probably be difficult to rule out at the moment.

I in fact wholly agree with you in saying that "philosophy of existence" is exposed to a double danger: either of falling into theology or of falling into abstraction. But the question that preoccupies me is not that of human existence; it is that of being as a whole and as such. And Nietzsche is no philosopher of existence either, but in his doctrine of the will and of the eternal return, he poses the ancient and unique question of being. But this question (which is only posed in *Sein und Zeit*) is not in any way addressed by Kierkegaard or by Nietzsche, and Jaspers in fact leaves it completely by the wayside.

But maybe these remarks themselves are too general a sketch to clarify the essential.

I am pleased to be able to reproduce this letter. It nevertheless remains the case that philosophy of existence is for Heidegger the necessary point of departure, if one wants to constitute a philosophy of being. I also ask myself what Heidegger contributes with regard to being itself. He says that it is time, with its three moments, its three ecstasies. But it is very difficult to isolate his thinking on this point about the being of the "existential" elements, for these three ecstasies define themselves by relation to Sorge.

Letter from Emmanuel Levinas

According to Monsieur Wahl, existential philosophy contains, *in fact*, a certain number of notions of theological origin. Kierkegaard presents them as such; Heidegger and Jaspers try to secularize them. These notions nevertheless play a considerable role in these philosophers, constituting the attraction of their thought, and assuring its connection with the concrete.

We can ask if the link between theology and existential philosophy is not, at the same time, more profound and—in relation to Heidegger—less determinative for existential philosophy than Monsieur Wahl says it is.

It is more profound on the condition of not limiting theology to the dogmatics of any positive religion. The problems to which dogmatics provides responses are independent and come into being from the simple fact of modern man's existence. For modern man, to exist is already to know solitude, death, and the need for salvation. When the soul doesn't know the consolation of the presence of God, it has a positive experience of his absence. Discourse on God does not lose its religious essence when it appears as a "discourse on the absence of God" or even as a silence about God. The religious is not ever totally out of the blue. What therefore links existential philosophy with theology is before all else its object itself—existence—a reality that if not theological is at least religious.

But, on the other hand, under the form that existential philosophy assumes in Heidegger, it banishes theology as far as possible. Moreover, irrespective of the part played by theology in Heidegger's intellectual formation, we can easily grant that, for him, to secularize a notion does not come down to camouflaging the religious aspect. Secularization must signify an operation that ends in truly surpassing the theological point of view. Therefore, the problem of the relation between Heidegger's philosophy and theology depends on the meaning that this secularization takes on. The point at which it carries itself out is indeed like the neuralgic point of his philosophy.

In the theological attitude one envisages things and beings in a manner that in Heideggerian terms it would be right to call *ontic*. One deals with *that* which is, with "beings" that fulfill their destiny. They are the object of narratives. They are treated as individuals and take part in a drama in which we are ourselves involved. Theology is essentially history and mythology. That is why in theological matters *authority* can guarantee truth.

The great concern of Heideggerian philosophy consists in showing at the base of man's *ontic* adventure that there is something more than a relation of a "being" to a "being," namely, the comprehension of being, ontology. The fate of human existence only interests Heidegger because of this ontology that it brings to completion. Heidegger thus breaks with theology to the exact extent that he makes the distinction between the ontic and the ontological (and he does this with a radicalism which is without precedent in the history of philosophy) and where fundamental transcendence fulfills itself for him not in the passage of one "being" to another, but from "being" to Being.

Under these conditions, it would be necessary to say that if Kierkegaard remains a theologian, this is not because he identified the transcendent with God rather than nature or the devil, but because he interpreted transcendence as contact with a "being." If Heidegger abandons the beyond, it is not because the *beyond* would be unknowable or "more theological" than the *below*, but because the very distinction between the beyond and the below is ontic and posterior to the ontological problem. Can we maintain that Heidegger constructs "the fall into the domain of the anonymous crowd" from the idea of sin? He seeks rather the ontological condition of the fall which is in fact ontic and of which original sin is a particular case (*Sein und Zeit*, § 40, n4). It always concerns finding the ontological conditions of different situations of actual existence, of passing from ontic and existent*ielle* understanding to understanding that he calls ontological and existen*tial*. Heidegger in any case sees this as the essence of his philosophical discovery. According to him (*Sein und Zeit*, § 45 n6), what remains foreign to Kierkegaard is the status of the problem of existence as an existen*tial* problem (by contrast to the existent*ielle*), in other words, the very perspective of ontology.

I would not willingly accept the idea that existence is by itself a religious reality. For me religion has the nature of a response. And existence has first of all the nature of a question.

*There are responses to this question other than religious; every engage-
ment, every risk, every decision, need not necessarily receive a religious
qualification.*

*I recognize that secularization in Heidegger is a surpassing, or in
any case a destruction, of the theological point of view.*

*And the observations of Monsieur Levinas permit us, I think, to draw
out the deeper meaning of Heidegger's reservations: the problem of being,
which he tells us is his problem, is the problem of being transposed from
the ontic domain to the existential domain (surely passing through the
existentielle domain). But what I don't see clearly is precisely what
the existential domain is. I fear that it is determined by the problem of
the conditions of the possibility of existence, a critique of existence, which
does not pose its questions in a more authentic or more adequate fashion
than the critique of reason, and which like it appeals to the formal idea
of "conditions of possibility." One of the questions to pose is to know how
Heidegger conceives of this idea of possibility, which plays such a great
role in his thought, as in that of Jaspers, and if he can give a definition or
a theory that allows for a nonformal concept.*

Letter from Karl Jaspers

A few weeks ago, you were good enough to send me your thesis
entitled "Subjectivity and Transcendence." I will confine my report to
what you said on the subject of my philosophy:

1. You wrote that my clarifications of limit situations assume
also, by the concept of limitation, the idea of a totality, that of the
Good and the True, but that my manner of thinking cannot, fundamentally, accept this totality. Now, nowhere do I maintain only that
there would be a knowledge of the totality of being; I admit only a
knowledge of diverse "modes of encompassing" in which the know-
able reveals itself to me each time in an original fashion. Each mode
of encompassing—firstly, real being, then consciousness as such,
then spirit, up to existence—encounters a limitation that is proper to
it, and in this way they reach the situation where, in another space,

the barrier can be broken up to the point that tranquillity would become possible in transcendence. This tranquillity, however, cannot be acquired by any act of knowledge. The limitation only exists therefore in relation to a mode of consciousness of being, but it is not absolute. Totality, in its turn, has several significations: that of perfection, of consistency, of the achievement of a harmony containing in itself unlimited connections; but totality also is only given each time in relation to a mode of encompassing. In transcendence, it ceases to be, as well as its contrary, since, there, all that is expressible is only inadequate metaphor.

2. Your saying that I find myself in opposition with Kierkegaard, in wanting to remain in this world here, which is proper to us, proffers a misunderstanding. It is true that I deny faith in a transcendence right where this faith does not manage to manifest itself, to reassure itself, to confirm itself in our world. I don't deny, however, the status of transcendence, and I am struck by finding myself before the "exception" that Kierkegaard saw within himself; I also believe I find myself before it as he would have wanted it: it is not an example for imitation, but it only serves to attract attention; it submits itself to the general principle of the "realization of itself in the world," like a standard it is aware of not satisfying, and that in constant ambiguity of either profound culpability or an amazing sense of being chosen for an irreplaceable and nonrepeatable uniqueness.

3. I would reject as dishonest every *Ersatz* of the idea of eternity by secularizing thought. The fact that, in the world, fidelity, continuity, "repetition" are a confirmation and an assurance of eternity, does not mean that they are substitutes for eternity; it means, not that eternity does not exist anymore, but that it founders for me if I no longer trust anyone, nor consequently in myself.

4. I would not deny that nostalgia for anything lost makes itself felt in my philosophy and that an echo of religion resounds in it. However, I think I can make out this echo in all philosophy that stands in the shadow of Plato and Kant, for whom a great nostalgia was the source of their investigation and of their vocation. Who among us would not wish, in the deepest part of our heart, that God would personally speak to him, as to a child—even if we know that the Divinity, in refusing

this to us, has given us precisely through that refusal the possibility of existing in our freedom *qua* human beings (Kant)?

5. That a "theory" of existence rightly sets aside existence itself is true for erroneous interpretations operating in the world in service of thoughts that clarify existence and summon us, as if they could subsume, know, and decide something in a concrete situation. Existentialism is the death of philosophy of existence, as it has always been ever since Plato's school. Philosophy can only awaken us.

6. As for "dangers," either from too close an attachment to theology, or of a too complete detachment from all "concreteness," I don't recognize these as dangers properly speaking. I would rather say: precisely what you designate as dangers I would want to get hold of at least as I understand it. Concerning "theology": what impresses itself on me as originally true, remains true, even when I understand that consequently, historically, it would probably not have entered my mind without Christianity. Concerning "concreteness": it is necessary that the philosophy rationally communicated remain in itself an open construction whose achievement is each time the affair of the thinker. It ought not to contain the concrete in the way the concrete is acquired in the sciences or communicable in the visions of poets, or in such a way as to remain historical in its very substance, and thereby available for each possible life. The greatest efforts of philosophical thought tend, it appears to me, to acquire not an empty concreteness but one that is authentic and effective. It is in this sense, for example, that we need to quit basing postulates and commandments on an anticipation of what they will decide on in history. Whoever communicates philosophically should adopt an attitude opposite to that of a dictator and do so by almost disappearing in an apparent flexibility and gentleness, and so reserving a space entirely free to the listener; if the listener doesn't go toward him, by philosophizing from his own resources, he would prefer to let him lose hope rather than offering him some pale imitation. What is more, we need to abandon, for example, "psychologizing" (among other concrete attitudes), which renders the abstract imaginable and denatures it precisely by doing so. Philosophy should seek to reach a degree of abstraction, which by its very form is capable of dealing with the most profound reality. Psychology—in our day, in

the form of psychoanalysis—is the doppelganger of philosophy. As soon as it involves itself with that, philosophy is lost. But, for almost every manifest form of philosophy, this psychological interpretation constitutes an erroneously drawn parallel. Indeed, concrete acts, all the philosopher's real doings, are indicative for the comprehension and examination of his philosophical thought. For philosophy is not, as is the case for science, a truth susceptible to being isolated. Down to the tone, down to the decisive nuance, one can recognize the thinker himself and what reflects itself in his entire life. However, psychological analysis—when psychoanalysis battles its adversary, not by substantial arguments, but by psychoanalyzing him—offers only a deformed image, already distorted at its origin. Yet, this deformed image is oriented to the truth: in philosophy, I work with the thoughts of another, such that thanks to those thoughts I come closer to the thinker himself, an encounter that is all the more profound the purer in form those thoughts become. "Concrete" analyses of my philosophy intend to be a crossing of the psychological in order to render intensely present possible existence.

7. You ask if Rimbaud, Van Gogh, Nietzsche, Kierkegaard are not more existential and essentially more philosophical than philosophy of existence. That a philosophy would be existential is, to tell the truth, an impossibility. Only a man, in his temporal being, is possible existence . . . I am content if I am one of those who you say are better off feeling the value of these very exceptions.

8. Combining Heidegger's name with mine, as if we are doing the same thing, exposes us both, it appears to me, to erroneous interpretations. What we have in common perhaps is a critical and negative attitude in regard to traditional university philosophy, along with a dependence on some of Kierkegaard's ideas. But what distinguishes us are the substantial contents where our respective philosophies come to birth.

There you have my succinct observations; I ask you to excuse their insufficient quality. In fact I have not at all perfectly understood the theses you sent to me. Because with each philosophical thought we enter into a network so inextricable from the multiplicity of possible interpretations that only a fortuitous encounter occasionally makes perceptible to us—for an instant and through the original project of thinking—the indubitable simplicity of truth.

I thank Karl Jaspers for the clarifications brought by his response. They are valuable to me. And what he said in numbers 5 and 7 marks, it seems to me, an agreement. I follow him less easily when in number 6 he radically condemns the work of psychoanalysis. He recognizes in number 2 that he denies faith in a transcendence that neither reassures itself nor confirms itself in our world. If I understand these expressions properly, it is thus that he admits on this point a difference between his thought and that of Kierkegaard in Fear and Trembling. *I think that what he says in paragraph 1 does not resolve the antinomy that exists in his philosophy between the idea of limitation as good and the idea of limitation as evil—or only resolves it with the help of distinctions that remain less than conceptual. Besides, is there perhaps knowledge of the diverse modes of the* Umgreifende? *Do we not find here the antinomy between breadth and narrowness that sheds light on existence? I would admit rather (and I think that he may admit this) that this is one of the essential tensions, one of these antinomies that clings to the very nature of being.*

I don't think I discern (as he says in number 4) in Kant, and a fortiori in Plato, nostalgia for a lost religious climate, for they still live in this climate. And their nostalgia is religious nostalgia rather than nostalgia for the religious. As for what he says in number 3, the question is precisely to know if one can at the time pose the question of "eternity for me" and truly believe in eternity. It founders for me, says Jaspers, but perhaps the believer in eternity founders before it, but doesn't see it as foundering "for him."

Observations of Hans Pollnow

In developing, by his very instructive exposition, certain fundamental problems related to the philosophy of existence (or, more precisely, in developing their "interrogation"), Jean Wahl is entitled to expect responses intended to complete his own considerations rather than bring objections to them. I permit myself thus to answer three among many important questions that he has raised and to add some personal arguments.

1. The distinction made by Wahl between "transascendence" and "transdescendence" seems to me one of incontestable philosophical fecundity, since not only does it differentiate the two forms under which every relation with transcendence concretizes itself, but also it usefully recalls, by these very terms, that transcendence, perceived too often as a *given* frozen in a sort of objectification, essentially signifies an existential *act* of the knowing subject. It thus concerns, as Wahl has formulated it, knowing if transascendence necessarily entails a movement toward goodness, and transdescendence, on the contrary, an inevitable direction toward evil.

I think that the human mind, in placing some phenomena above, others below, according to a cosmic spatial order of values, both in philosophical interpretations and in religious conceptions of the world, only translates, through this primordial symbolism, a transcendental schema, so to speak, from its own "anthropological" structure. This schema, verifiable by our phenomenological consciousness, is transcendental because it ties both the phenomenality and the intelligibility of the world to a certain system of nonmetaphorical, but actual, directions; it is anthropological because it expresses precisely the primitive attitude of the human being toward all other beings together with the world in general, an attitude establishing in man's rationality his "superiority" by relation to the rest of creation.

It thus appears to me that the process of rationalization is originally seen as a sort of ascent toward the light (we speak as well of the dawning of the day), and on the other hand as a return for man, who "ascends," thanks to knowledge of the self and of the universe, to what remains unknown or even unknowable appearing as a descent toward the darkness or, in other words, as the falling of night. But it is only to the extent that the good is coordinated, in a philosophy, with the brightness of the rational and evil consequently with the obscurity of the irrational, essentially elementary in its force and impenetrable in its structure, that the good places itself on high and evil down below in the hierarchy of essential or moral values. The proof is that every conception of the world identifying the good with the irrational and rightly conceiving rationality as bad, implies the necessity of a transdescendence toward the good, for example in Goethe's "Faust" under the form of "descent toward the realm of the Mothers" or that of a transascendence toward the evil, as is the case in the philosophy of Klages, who considers the spirit the irreconcilable enemy of the soul and of all essential and creative force. Besides, for a thought placing the good in the lower regions, it goes without saying that the pejorative and negative meaning of the below effaces itself by transforming into a positive meaning of depth, such that we find, for example, most explicitly in Romanticism.

2. I don't see why all philosophy of existence, desirous of maintaining itself in close contact with concrete and specific facts in the historicity of life, should necessarily bear the characteristic of a theology. It appears to me that a fundamental difference exists between theological thought and philosophical thought, in this case, philosophy of religion. If both envisage the same data, they do so under very distinct aspects.

The certitude of the data forming the content of religion and thus constituting the point of departure for the theologian is only, for a philosophy of religion, an outcome, and by that very outcome, the crowning achievement of constructive thought. Let's consider, from this angle, the function that proof for the existence of God enjoys, on the one hand, in the theological conception of the world, and on the other hand, in that of philosophy.

On the theological level, the need for resorting to a proof of the existence of God signals a crisis in religious consciousness, a crisis due to the dynamism of destructive rationalization that never holds back, all the more so when it comes to transcendence; it is thus to reassure itself in that transcendence that thought tries to search for proofs for the existence of God, proofs consequently bearing an *apologetic* character.

Quite to the contrary, on the philosophical level, proofs of the existence of God fulfill an essentially different function: they don't serve an apologetic goal, but they participate in the accomplishment of a *constructive* effort of a philosophy of the totality, in translating the audacious élan of a thought sure enough of itself to transcend its proper limits and also support proof of the improvable.

That a concrete philosophy of existence can take, in its evolution, a religious turn, appears to me an indubitable and inevitable consequence. But why is it necessary to see a theological turn inherent to existentialism, that is to say, the abandonment of confidence in thought directed and controlled by itself, such that it represents the only authentically philosophical attitude? For this religious perspective is not intended, in my view, to reassure a weakened faith and bring a threatened existence back toward transcendence. I would consider precisely the most perfect attempt at a genuine conquest of transcendence and the veritable foundation of a free communication of subjectivity believing in transcendence, under the form of a philosophy of religion.

3. The problem of existence is firstly that of the possibility of realizing existence. Wherever the limits of this possibility don't make themselves felt, existence cannot become problematic in itself and cannot form the object, or, to put it better, the content of a philosophy of existence. Existence is expressed then by forms other than those of the existent being's on existence. But at the basis of all existential thought consciousness finds itself with a limited possibility of realizing existence. It is precisely there that the essential difference resides between *Rimbaud* and *Van Gogh*, on the one hand, and the philosophers of existence on the other, like *Kierkegaard, Nietzsche, Jaspers,* and *Heidegger.* For it is only the experienced limitation of existence susceptible to being realized that admits of representing, in a philosophy, that which is problematic in the essence of existence. Some live existence without thinking under the forms of the philosophy of existence; the lives that they realize carry an exemplary and *apodictic* character. For others, existence presents itself as an existential *problem,* thus providing them with material for reflection and guiding them toward the deployment of existential thought in a philosophy of existence.

In the course of the discussion on Wahl's paper, a distinction between existential philosophy and philosophy of existence was proposed, but I don't see the legitimacy of this distinction. I don't understand how this antithesis can advance us in the development of problems otherwise than by revealing to us that we ought to abandon those problems that have been established for us in the first place. This distinction has been used to establish a sort of gradation of philosophers according to their value, by placing, for example, *Kierke-gaard* and *Nietzsche*, existential philosophers, on a higher rank to that of *Jaspers* and *Heidegger*, simple philosophers of existence. Such an evaluation appears to me totally arbitrary, since there is no reason to suppose that a philosophy of existence cannot be just as existential as any other philosophy. Of course I accept the characterization of *Jaspers's* and *Heidegger's* philosophies as philosophies of existence. But is the term *existential philosophy* anything other than a tautology? Allow me to examine still more closely the antithesis of these notions. All genuine and authentic philosophy, and *Jaspers* has emphasized this, can only be existential philosophy. It is precisely this existentiality that makes a thought, fundamentally, philosophical. It means that all genuinely philosophical thought is essentially existential or that all existential thought becomes philosophy as soon as it finds a systematic form. So why translate, by a tautological formula, that which constitutes the very essence of philosophy as such and which doesn't distinguish it from philosophy of existence, for which it is just as valid, but from all incidental and harmless thought in relation to existence?

One could perhaps explain more precisely the difference that, in my opinion, exists not between the philosophy called "existential" and philosophy of existence, but rather between philosophy as such and philosophy of existence. To this end, it is necessary to realize the fact that all philosophy deserving this name is essentially existential by a transparency to the existence of the philosopher who *illumines himself* in it, and that philosophy of existence (philosophy no less existential, on the condition that it would be truly philosophical) has a double relation with existence *qua* philosophy, for existence *illumines itself* in it, and *qua* thought concerning existence, for so it *illumines* existence.

I think then that the antithesis breaks down, since the term *existential philosophy* annihilates itself entirely by its tautological nature, whereas philosophy of existence remains a framework wide enough to encompass *Kierkegaard* and *Nietzsche* as much as *Jaspers* and *Heidegger*.

I heartily accept the penetrating remarks that Pollnow has made in number 1, where he simultaneously puts in doubt the idea of a transascendence toward evil and thinks that analysis of the ideas of good and evil, begun with Nietzsche, has never been truly continued.

I have not said that all philosophy of existence ought to take the character of theology. And I tried to see how it could be freed from every religious idea. Pollnow wants on the contrary to show that its separation from religious ideas would diminish its vitality and maybe even be a symptom of death; he seeks to distinguish the function of the idea of transcendence in the religious man and in the philosopher. But doubtless he doesn't take sufficient account of the fact that its function in the philosopher is explained because it takes place in an ebb of religious thought, at religion's low tide. What he calls "the real conquest of transcendence, the foundation of free communication," is often only the reversal of a movement of weakened and anguished faith.

I think that for Van Gogh or Rimbaud, existence has been a problem, although they haven't exposited this problem primarily through reflection, but in their work and their life. They also have had an existence of limited possibilities, although it can be maintained that they have been able to realize themselves in their work in a more complete fashion than philosophers have been able to do in theirs. (It still remains a question. And Maine de Biran offers the example of a philosopher who remains a problem, who remains limited, and expresses himself in a work and a life that express this fully, precisely through their dissatisfied and unachieved nature.)

Despite the objections of Pollnow, I think that there is something useful and true in the distinction proposed by Berdyaev between existential philosophy and philosophy of existence. The case of Nietzsche and of Kierkegaard, that of Socrates, maybe that of Descartes and of Kant, these are examples of philosophies that are sources of themselves—even if one can enumerate their influences.

Letter from Jeanne Hersch

Apropos of the idea of repetition, of theories of the instant or those of the eternal return: is it right to see these as an *"Ersatz"* of the idea of eternity? *"Ersatz"* is strongly pejorative, suggesting that it concerns the same thing, but "in counterfeit," without any compensation for its lost authenticity. But it appears to me that repetition, the instant, the eternal return, are projections, or translations, of eternity on the human level. Authenticity is only lost in appearance, and only when the translation is allowed to pass for the original. For my part, I am inclined even to think that authenticity is better protected by the attempts at translation than by the pure divine term. For we are human beings, and thus a nexus of forces and a crossing of paths, and I don't think that one of these paths can be authentic *for us* without implicating the others. The divine end can only discover its authenticity for us by incarnating itself in our life and our thought laden with the body. Besides, we hardly recognize it in its purity but by its irreducible resistance to this human effort of incarnation. And doubtless there you have the function of these notions "repetition," "instant," "eternal return." Is this the role of an *Ersatz*? I don't think so.

Apropos of the more or less religious character of existential philosophy: I don't think that either Heidegger, or Jaspers in any case, would deny it. Jaspers in no way seeks to eliminate it, and although he yet forcefully opposes his philosophy to all theology, it appears to me that he does so first and foremost because of a refusal: the refusal to speak of God as if he were given. You can ever only speak of the search for him. The "more or less" that I wrote at the beginning of this paragraph is pretty stupid, in short, because of the relative element that it introduces here: in one sense, this philosophy is absolutely religious since God is sought there and nothing else; in another sense, it absolutely is not because it refuses to speak of God as a revealed being. So, here again, there is a refusal to leave the human condition, because of the certitude that a man has no path of piety other than a human path, for his thought and his acts. But transcendence remains transcendent— whence the sense of a limit, of a failure, of all negative notions, not because of tragic love, but really because man is human, clearly.

The double danger you spoke of, theology or abstraction, appears to be one that definitely is a threat to existential philosophy. But this observation appears to me to prove its truth, its exact coincidence with the human condition: for I think that man, whatever he does, never definitively escapes from this double danger. There is no shelter against it, and to try to secure yourself against it is to have already given up. We have to be escaping it throughout our life or thought.

That some lives can be more existential and more philosophical than the philosophies of existence, there I fully agree with you, and Jaspers does too I think. (How many times have I heard him emphasize: "But philosophy is still not existence: it is a possibility of existence."). And, doubtless not only Rimbaud, Van Gogh, and Nietzsche, but some very obscure lives. Yet existential philosophy appears to me to do more than make us feel their value: it is a call, maybe more direct for some, and in any case different, having grasped others differently. Can there be too many calls, too many kinds of call?

I see nothing to respond to in this strong letter, except that the reader of Jaspers does not always stay at the level where Mlle Hersch would want to keep him, and that, appropriately, this philosophy—but maybe this is the destiny of all philosophy of this type—can appear too difficult, by reason of the negative theology at its summit; or too easy, by the fact that the unknown God can be attained in multiple ways, and that we can always say, in one way or another, that God is attained in his ciphers and through historicity. It seems to me that this sentiment, comparable to my own, is expressed in the following letter that Mme Bespaloff has generously written to me.

Letter from Rachel Bespaloff

In short, what keeps me away from Jaspers's philosophy is that it is far too convenient for me, that nothing in it wounds or offends me. Despite everything, it is a philosophy of defeat—we are ourselves defeats . . . Essentially, its last word is: suffering. I know it well, alas! that *durch dulden besteht die Welt* [the world is made up of suffering], I know it only too well. But is being convenient the first and last value?

Take the chapter on liberty in the second volume. It appears that all Jaspers's gifts—his marvelous penetration, his conceptual clarity, including even the perfect probity of his mind—turn against him.

While reading these pages, I approve of everything, and I have no objection to raise. But, when I arrive at the end of the chapter, I have the impression of a disaster: Freedom is no more, it never was. What happened to it?

Nietzsche, even when he denies it, renders it present to me—and this is not a freedom wedged between the conditioned necessity of *Dasein* and the unconditioned necessity of transcendence. It is the truth—and I would not know how to tell you how I recognize it. Why, consequently, would I agree with Jaspers, even when he confirms my own experience, rather than with the revelations of Nietzsche?

Es ist genug dass Sein ist [It is enough that being is]: doubtless Nietzsche says nothing else (even though he avoids the word *being*), but with such a tone, such an accent . . . That changes everything. The danger, for existential philosophy, is not, it seems to me, of linking itself too closely to the religious, it is of not tearing away from the ethical. Jaspers only pulls it off, in my opinion, by a transfiguration that is *poetic*, in the broadest sense of the word. For all in all, what is the "cipher," except (under a new term still charged with magic) the transmutation of the apparent phenomenon where the unresolved meaning of being unfolds itself?

What enriches me in Jaspers's philosophy is what it rightly struggles to put in the background: the depth and acuity of the psychological intuition that is perhaps, at the origin, a poetical intuition of temporality: the knowledge of man.

Letter from Karl Löwith

I think that Kierkegaard has destroyed, rather than vivified, philosophical conceptions. And as for Jaspers and Heidegger, I always had the impression that there was a paradox here; for Jaspers's philosophy is essentially an *Ersatz* of religion, although Jaspers would be himself essentially a philosopher of antitheological enlightenment, whereas on the contrary, the philosophy of Heidegger is anti-Christian, although— or precisely because—he remains essentially a theologian. In Jaspers, "the echo of the religious" is no longer present except under the form of an existentialist Kantianism. In Heidegger, one still feels in his work an immediate religious impulse, but a perverted one.

Letter from Käte Nadler

Käte Nadler, who opposes existentialist philosophy from a Hegelian point of view, writes that she is in agreement with me on the double danger to which existential philosophy is exposed, which she herself signals in an article from Tatwelt.

Letter from Denis de Rougemont

Why do you want—or they want—philosophy to be purified of theology? Theology certainly deserves the name of science. It is even a much less variable science than the so-called exact sciences, the foundations of which are overturned every twenty years, from top to bottom.

I don't think that transcendence can ever be "simply nature." You see it in Goethe, in Tolstoy, in Nietzsche: to the extent that there is an element of transcendence, nature becomes divinity (and it has to be this way). For my part, I don't perceive the concrete relation to transcendence wherever the feeling of the divine, of the sacred, would be lacking. But your paper usefully orients us toward a new analysis of transcendence in its relation to powers of imagination and not only in its relation to ethics.

Letter from Louis Lavelle

I would ask simply if, in the ambiguity of the divine and the demonic, or of the transascendent and transdescendent, the ambiguity that is in the very heart of anxiety, there is a principle of distinction that precisely causes there to be an ambiguity here and which is where this principle of distinction comes from. For it could be the effect of prejudice or, on the contrary, an exigency of consciousness, of the very act by which it constitutes itself, in which case it would consequently be a matter of searching for an ontological foundation.

I very willingly admit that the distinction between the divine and the demonic (influenced by theological and moral conceptions) and that of the transascendent and transdescendent would have to be kept separate, more so than I have done in my summary. The ambiguity does not thereby disappear; but perhaps one could see that it no longer appears except when ideas from a different origin are superimposed onto investigations of a metaphysical nature.

This is also more or less how I would respond to Raymond Aron.

Letter from Raymond Aron

Allow me to submit to you the following reflections:

You want to separate existential philosophy from the moral categories of good and evil, of above and below; you speak of transcendence without attaching to this term any shade of value. That being so, I perceive very well the difficulty of introducing into existential philosophy, such as you conceive it, the abstract notions of ethics or of religion. But what then do you have left in order to describe metaphysically lived experiences? What does transcendence signify, and *a fortiori*, transascendence and transdescendence? You say you renounce these words that signify effort in order to rise up, or, on the contrary, to sink down. But are you sure you respect lived experience this way? Doesn't transcendence disappear if nature stops being the goal of transcendence toward the below? Is it not according to religious or moral categories, that these experiences define themselves, constitute themselves? So much so that your supposed faithfulness would express an arbitrary interpretation of these existing lives; I will call the interpretation you propose to us your aesthetic skepticism.

Indeed what value would you retain, having abstracted from good and evil, from spirit and nature, from God and the demon, in order to single out philosophical lives? That of intensity: the most intense existences, the most problematic, would be the most philosophical. I confess that I see in this a sort of amoralism and irrationalism, the psychological meaning of which I know better than the philosophical meaning. Wouldn't the neurotic become the most philosophical, since who is more torn down than him? Isn't the experience of destruction, of war, at least as intense as the experience of the philosopher who contemplates transcendence? You end up judging Rimbaud or Van Gogh more philosophical than the philosophers of existence. There again I find the bad conscience of the philosopher (in France) who feels himself inferior to the artist or the poet. In a sense, you may be right. If it's about human greatness, Rimbaud is perhaps more important than all professors of philosophy, but I fear that such a question would be nonsensical. Why compare some types or others of human beings? Souls are incomparable. Your hierarchy translates some personal preferences, and I ask if the very idea of such a hierarchy is not spiritually sacrilegious (doesn't God refuse to distribute prizes or fix ranks this way?). In any case, it exceeds the possibilities of our human understanding.

On the other hand, if we take philosophy in the strict sense, it seems to me that you are evidently wrong, for to experience intensely the philosophical drama, the problem of destiny, is perhaps to reveal a philosophical temperament, the condition of all philosophy. But, to the extent that these people don't express their drama, or they express it in images or in verse, they are not philosophers or at the least they are only in the eyes of the philosopher who, in reflecting on his experience, perceives there the mark of what he and he alone determines as philosophy, because he is capable of describing conceptually, ethically, religiously that which would otherwise remain on the level of experience.

I fear that your alternative would be imprecise and that there would be means of easily avoiding both theology and abstraction. I don't see why theology in itself would risk compromising existential philosophy. In order to be authentic, theology has no need to reject every borrowing in its doctrines. We know very well that mystical experiences are penetrated by the religious thought in which they participate. Existential philosophers are rather well united in a human universe that they imagine they are renewing by the fact that they live intensely either the antinomies or the fundamental data. But the more they are existential the less they are philosophers: not because they are theologians but because they confine themselves to expressing a previously established system, without demonstrating its validity, or situating themselves by reflection in the totality of human life.

As for the philosophies of existence, they no doubt slip into abstraction if, in the manner of Jaspers, they retain existential categories by formalizing them and would aim at the paradox of standing at the same time at both the level of existence and at the level of reflection. In this case, indeed, they would speak of a decision—without being precise on this—they deny the truth of philosophy altogether by linking up judgments that pretend to the truth. Abstract theory of man's metaphysical situation: that's more or less the theme of Jaspers's philosophy, but in such a way that this theory is contradictory, for this theory isn't lived through; in fact, we either think the life that we chose or we think concrete human life such that it unfolds itself across history. And, in this last case, all of Jaspers's philosophy is only the introduction to a philosophical comprehension of human history and of the human being. In other words, one cannot stand in a philosophy of existence (of Jaspers's type), but the same goes for indicating the alternative of theology and abstraction. For from the moment that you have not chosen the first term, you have chosen the second, and since you recognize the danger of abstraction, you recognize in a single stroke the necessity of going beyond abstract theory of choice toward a comprehension of the concrete human being and maybe beyond, toward philosophy of being or, in any case, of the human being and being for man. The path of philosophy opens with the phenomenology of existences.

I do not think that one can say that I accord to the word transcendence *"no shade of value" or that I separate existential philosophy from the notions of above and below—of "elevating" and "lowering" unless they are taken in a purely moral sense (of good and of evil). I concede very readily that nature would be the goal of transcendence toward the below. (I am taking over Aron's expressions in order to better indicate what I don't accept in the thesis that he ascribes to me.)*

I am not conscious of having this philosopher's bad conscience that Aron attributes to French philosophers. On the contrary, I take the word philosopher *in a very broad sense. I considered Rimbaud, Van Gogh, as "sources of philosophy": and I would like to add that the source has a purity that its rivers do not; in the second place, it is perhaps owing to a slightly scholarly conception of philosophy that I have not dared to call them philosophers.*

Aron says that the hierarchy exceeds the possibilities of our intellect; no doubt, but the question of the intellect is one for him to answer. For me, it is the question of an arbitrary evaluation: I want then to say I am the only arbiter.

I refuse the idea of a superiority of the one who would describe conceptually, ethically, religiously over the one who would otherwise remain at the level of experience. I note that by the words "only it is capable of . . ." and "level of experience" Aron establishes a hierarchy. Not that he would tell us about this though—isn't there something sacrilegious about that according to him?

For me, here there is even less of the sacrilegious than the sacred; it is not philosophy because it is reflection, but what I have called the source of philosophy (or philosophy in the sense that I would like to give to this word), or even the hard kernel, impenetrable to reflection, that is at the root of all great works.

And therefore I don't see in what I tried to express the effect of an aesthetic system, but an affirmation of the passion to see transcendence from the term of the movement of transcendence in relation to our conceptual thought and its immanence in the intensity of experience.

I believe I can also put Lavelle's letter close to Bastide's.

Letter from Georges Bastide

The meditation on the adventure of Kierkegaardian thought is full of instruction for philosophy, and since you characterize this thought by the junction of a tensed and anxious subjectivity with an anxiety-provoking transcendence, I think that you deeply grasp the dramatic nub. However, I have, on my own account, interpreted this drama across a duality of slightly different terms.

1. Subjectivity and transcendence only seem to me to be an effect of the realist usage of the concept of existing Unity in its double application to the subject and the object.

Applied to the subject, the concept of existing Unity gives birth to the concept of *unicity*: the subject is thought as a punctual unity; in space, it would be like the center of a sphere from which emanates an infinity of rays; in time, it is the instant where the past closes itself off and the future opens itself up.

Applied to the object, the concept of existent Unity gives birth to the concept of *totality*: the object is thought as a synthetic unity; in space, it is the indefinitely multiple flourishing of rays from the sphere; in time, it is the retrospective or prospective projection of the infinite multiplicity of possibilities.

The relation of the subject to the object is thus, for realist thought, the opposition of unicity to totality. It is because there is no object without subject, nor subject without object, that there is in all thought a "junction" of subjective unicity and transcendent totality.

2. This double acceptance of the existing Unity creates for realist thought, which poses the object in itself and the subject in itself, a fundamental antinomy where this thought irrecoverably stumbles.

In a totally general fashion first, the position of absolute existence of one of the terms causes the existence of the other to vanish into nothingness, for the absolute existence of the unicity is the negation of the multiple, and the absolute existence of the totality is on the contrary its affirmation. To pose the Being of the totality is to affirm the existence of the multiple and deny the existence of the unique; but to pose the Being of the One is to affirm the existence of the unique and deny that of the whole multiple. It is precisely the old Parmenidean problem.

One could follow the antinomy across the categories of space and time (Jaspers's "communication" and "historicity") where each of the terms would still reveal its subversive power by relation to the other.

To establish as absolute the unicity of the center of the sphere is to destroy the sphere, which only has existence by the multiplicity of its rays; but to establish as absolute the synthetic totality of the sphere is to destroy the existence in itself of the center, which is only the convergence of the rays.

In time, to set up absolutely the unicity of the instant is to destroy the existence of multiple "befores" and "afters"; but to affirm the existence of the multiples is to cause the instant, which becomes a simple limit, to vanish.

So, each time the subject wants to settle down in its unicity, totality loses existence, and this subject finds itself face-to-face with the Nothing ("To exist, Heidegger says, in fact comes down to this: to be maintained within nothingness," *Bifur*, 1931, p. 15).[12]

The transcendence of the whole can only be thought then by a subject who loses the unicity of its existence. The subjectivity of the Unique can only think the transcendence of the Nothing like an object.

3. It is from there that anxiety is born. The presence of theological and moral elements results from the constant equation of Being and Value in all metaphysical realists. Being and the Good are there identical, and the judgments of reality of such a metaphysics are always judgments of value. It is why the antinomy becomes tragic and anxious.

The subjective Unique can only guard its being, that is to say its value, by opposing itself to a nothing of totality, that is to say a Nothing of transcendent value. Inversely, one can pose the transcendent existence of total Value only by denying the being and thus the value of the Unique. What results is that every gain of value for the subjective would be a loss of value for the transcendent. The "transascendence" of the subject is a "transdescendence" of the object, and vice versa. Man and God would endlessly trade back and forth the demonic accusation.

4. This fundamental antinomy constitutes the ultimate "barrier," as Dostoyevsky felt it, against which realist thought is shattered. The Kierkegaardian moment is the *nec plus ultra* of this thought.

Realist thought indeed cannot transcend the duality of the subject and object. That is why it can't think its way to a subsequent stage: Every attempt at overcoming, as Hegel called it, is taken up in the rebirth

---

12. [Bastide refers here to Corbin's translation of Heidegger's *Was ist Metaphysik?* which appeared in an issue of *Bifur* (June 1931).]

of this antinomy, which is always the very same. Only the nostalgic thought of an impossible return or a negation of all thought (Dostoyevsky's "becoming deliberately foolish") can make an appearance.

5. Realist consciousness can have then, at the base of its misfortune, the revelation of its essential perversion. That is what it translates by the idea of a fall that has radically separated it from Being.

But it can see also that, in a parallel perspective, the thought of Being is irremediably forbidden to it. Realist thought cannot be existential, for it carries in itself a power that dissolves all existence, which it wants to take hold of.

All that is left for this "perverted" thought to do is to "convert" itself to the idealist attitude, which moves in exactly an inverse sense.

The subject and object cease to be opposition in order to become relation. The relational Unity, unifying unity, escapes the antinomy of the Unique and the Total; and the act of valorizing thought coincides there exactly with the genesis of spiritual being.

I feel especially far from the thought of the last paragraph, at the moment where Bastide presents the idealist doctrine as a remedy. But he wanted to specify his position in a way that diminishes the distance I sense between us.

Second Letter from Georges Bastide

By idealism, I in no way understand a vision of the world that would be able to furnish to the mind once and for all the rest and the homeland that it searches for. I understand only the attitude of investigation and the direction of effort that find their departure and their orientation in consciousness's grasp of the preeminence of the spiritual, and that are at the origin of all the works of the spirit.

I think that this attitude is never able to be achieved right away, that it can only rise up in the midst of the fragments of tragic realist consciousness, and even that the profundity of idealist thought, insofar as it produces value, is a function of the profundity of tragedy that has been achieved in realist thought. I would say even that as he writes a work where the tragic is thought, Kierkegaard is already implicitly in the idealist attitude since there is in his act the affirmation that thought of tragedy is superior, by rights, to tragedy that thinks.

Maybe these hasty reflections would permit you to find my thought less removed from yours.[13]

13. [I note here that the final letter present in the text from the *Bulletin* ([1937]: 209–11) does not appear in the book, which closes with Bastide's second letter. This excised letter, by Raymond Lenoir, receives no response from Wahl unlike the others. That letter suggests (I summarize) that this meeting is evidence of a worldwide, transformational movement in philosophy gathering steam in "Italy, Germany, Poland, and Russia," and assumes therefore that the "*existencielle* [*sic*] *philosophie*" discussed is only an instantiation of vitalism and its renewed concentration on the essential, the "*sentiment de vie*," or, later in the letter, the "*sens de la vie*," that broke open on the French scene with Biran and Ravaisson in the nineteenth century and was continued by Bergson in the twentieth. It is this *sens de la vie* that is, for Lenoir, clearly a student of Bergson, the secret reality behind every domain of appearing and meaning.]

APPENDIX 1

Selected List of Philosophers, Artists, and Poets in Wahl's Text

Alexander, Samuel (1859–1958). Metaphysician and philosopher of science; influence on A. N. Whitehead; first Jewish fellow of a college of Oxford University; author of *Space, Time and Deity* (1920), his (1916–18) Gifford Lectures.

Aristippus (mid-5th–mid-4th c. BC). Student of Socrates; typically conceived as advocating a moderate hedonism.

Arnauld, Antoine (1612–1694). Theologian, philosopher, mathematician, and influential public intellectual; author of *On Frequent Communion* (1643) and *The Art of Thinking*, commonly known as *The Port-Royal Logic* (1683).

Béguin, Albert (1901–1957). Swiss thinker and author of *L'âme romantique et le rêve, essai sur le romantisme allemand et la poésie française* (1937/39).

Biran, Maine de (1766–1824). Philosopher and key originator of French vitalism and spiritualism; a major influence on Felix Ravaisson and later Michel Henry.

Bosanquet, Bernard (1848–1923). English neo-Hegelian; author of *Philosophical Theory of the State* (1899) and *The Meeting of Extremes in Contemporary Philosophy* (1921).

Boutroux, Émile (1845–1921). Philosopher of science influenced by Maine de Biran; advocated the compatibility of science and religion; a member of the Académie française and author of *Science and Religion in Contemporary Philosophy* (Gifford Lectures, 1903–5).

Bradley, F. H. (1846–1924). Author of *Appearance and Reality* (1893); with Bosanquet Bradley was a so-called Absolute Idealist.

Brandès, Georg (1842–1927). Influential Danish author and critic; author of *Main Currents in Nineteenth-Century Literature* (6 vols.; 1906).

Brémond, Henri (1865–1933). Member of the Académie française and author of *Histoire littéraire du sentiment religieux en France depuis la fin des guerres de religion jusqu'à nos jours* (11 vols.; 1916–36).

Broglie, Louis de (1892–1987). French physicist and Nobel Prize laureate; conceived of the wave-particle duality thesis.

Chénier, André (1762–1794). Poet; precursor to Romanticism; he was executed by guillotine during the French Revolution.

Corbin, Henri (1903–1978). Philosopher and historian of Islamic mystical thought; early translator of Heidegger and author of *Creative Imagination in the Sufism of Ibn ʾArabi* (1969).

Corte, Marcel de (1905–1994). Catholic philosopher and critic of modern society.

Courbet, Gustave (1819–1877). Controversial French painter; leader of nineteenth-century Realism.

Damascius (AD mid-5th–mid-6th c.). Syrian philosopher; head of the School of Athens when it was shut down by Justinian in 529; known as the "last pagan philosopher" or the "last of the Neoplatonists." His central theme is divine incomprehensibility, as can be seen in his masterwork, *Problems and Solutions Concerning First Principles.*

Eddington, Sir Arthur (1882–1944). British astrophysicist and philosopher of science.

Empedocles (5th c. BC). Pre-Socratic philosopher; author of the influential theory of the four elements, which can be found in the extant fragments of his great poem *On Nature.*

Estève, Claude-Louis (1890–1933). Philosopher and literary critic; author of *Études philosophiques sur l'expression littéraire* (1938).

Fernandez, Ramon (1894–1944). Mexican-born French writer and critic; author of *De la personnalité* (1928) and the novel *Le Pari* (1932).

Gide, André (1869–1951). French Symbolist and anticolonialist writer; he received the Nobel Prize in literature in 1947.

Granet, Marcel (1884–1940). French sociologist and ethnologist; applied Durkheim's thought to the study of Chinese civilization.

Hamelin, Octave (1856–1907). Philosopher influenced by Durkheim; he wrote books on Descartes, Aristotle, and the "neocritical" idealist Charles Renouvier.

Hartmann, Nicolai (1882–1950). Eastern European philosopher; student of neo-Kantian thinkers Hermann Cohen and Paul Natorp; author of *Possibility and Actuality* (1938).

Holt, Edwin B. (1873–1946). American philosopher and psychologist; student of William James and author of *The Concept of Consciousness* (1918).

Huxley, Thomas Henry (1825–1895). English biologist known as "Darwin's bulldog"; coined the term *agnostic* in self-conscious opposition to the term *gnostic*; grandfather of writer Aldous Huxley.

Klages, Ludwig (1872–1956). German philosopher, poet, and psychologist; a protoexistentialist, he advocated a quasi-Romantic mysticism of earth and antiquity; a fundamental distinction of his is between *Geist* (mind) and *Seele* (soul), which negate and affirm life, respectively (*Der Geist als Widersacher der Seele*, 1929).

Lamartine, Alphonse de (1790–1869). French Romantic poet, novelist, playwright, and political personality during the French Revolution; author of *Méditations poétiques* (1820).

Leconte de Lisle, Charles-Marie-René (1818–1894). French poet of the "Parnassian" movement (a sort of proto-Symbolism) and member of the Académie française; translator of Greek tragedians.

Melissus of Sardis (5th c. BC). Pre-Socratic philosopher; student of Parmenides; last of the Eleatics.

Montague, William Pepperell (1873–1953). American philosopher; critic of English-speaking Idealism; author of *The New Realism* (1912).

Montherlant, Henry de (1895–1972). French writer and member of the Académie française; author of the novel *Les célibataires* (1934).

Musset, Alfred de (1810–1857). French poet, playwright, novelist; author of *La Confession d'un enfant du siècle* (1836).

Nerval [Gérard Labrunie] (1808–1855). Poet; central figure in French Romanticism; author of the novel *Sylvie* (1853).

Pater, Walter (1839–1904). English essayist, historian, novelist; one of the great prose stylists of the nineteenth century; author of *The Renaissance: Studies in Art and Poetry* (1873) and *Marius the Epicurian* (1885).

Patmore, Coventry (1823–1896). English poet; author of *The Angel in the House* (1854).

Perry, Ralph Barton (1876–1957). American "neo-Realist" philosopher; student of William James; author of *Realms of Value* (Gifford Lectures, 1948–50) and the Pulitzer Prize–winning *The Thought and Character of William James* (1935).

Powys, John Cowper (1872–1963). British poet, novelist and philosopher; author of *In Defense of Sensuality* (1930) and *A Glastonbury Romance* (1932); Wahl dedicates a chapter to Powys's thought in his *Poésie, pensée, perception* (1948).

Racine, Jean (1639–1699). Playwright and major figure in French letters, primarily known for his tragedies.

Rauh, Frédéric (1861–1909). French moral philosopher; teacher of René Le Senne; taught that moral ideas cannot be analyzed when abstracted from moral experience; considered by some to be the (true) father of French existentialism.

Raymond, Marcel (1897–1981). Swiss literary critic influenced by phenomenology (of the "Geneva School"); author of *De Baudelaire au surréalisme* (1933).

Reid, Thomas (1710–1796). Scottish philosopher of common sense; fierce opponent of David Hume; author of *An Inquiry into the Human Mind on the Principles of Common Sense* (1764).

Renéville, Rolland de (1903–1962). French poet and essayist; author of *L'expérience poétique, ou le feu secret du langage* (1938) and *Rimbaud le voyant* (1929).

Royce, Josiah (1855–1916). American philosopher of the school of Objective Idealism (which identifies all reality with the perception of it in God); influenced by C. S. Peirce and William James; author of *The Spirit of Modern Philosophy* (1892).

Saint-Martin, Louis-Claude de (1743–1803). French esoteric thinker influenced by Boehme.

Santayana, George (1863–1952). Spanish-American philosopher of a pragmatist bent (Idealism is true but is of no consequence since thinking is not detached from our animal needs); author of influential multivolume works such as *The Life of Reason* (5 vols.; 1905–6) and *The Realms of Being* (4 vols.; 1927–40), which builds on his *Scepticism and Animal Faith* (1923).

Saurat, Denis de (1890–1958). French scholar with a strong interest in Blake (e.g., *Blake and Modern Thought*, 1929), and the poetic dimensions of philosophy and vice versa (e.g., *Milton, Man and Thinker*, 1920/25).

Sellars, Roy Wood (1880–1973). American philosopher critical of the mechanistic view of nature in light of evolutionary theory; author of *Evolutionary Naturalism* (1922); father of philosopher Wilfred Sellars.

Sheldon, Wilmon Henry (1875–1981). American process philosopher; author of *Process and Polarity* (1944) and *God and Polarity: A Synthesis of Philosophies* (1954).

Spencer, Herbert (1820–1903). Victorian-era English philosopher and social scientist; developed an early account of evolution as the key to understanding everything; the phrase "survival of the fittest" is Spencer's.

Strong, Charles Augustus (1862–1940). American philosopher who lived in Florence; student of William James, close associate of Santayana; counted among the American Critical Realists.

Swedenborg, Emanuel (1688–1772). Swedish scientist and inventor; receiver of bizarre revelations of the spiritual worlds; author of *Heaven and Hell* (1758).

Swinburne, Algernon Charles (1837–1909). English "decadent" poet, dramatist, and critic; author of *Atalanta in Calydon* (1865) and *Poems and Ballads* (1866).

Theophrastus (late 4th–late 3rd c. BC). Successor of Aristotle as scholarch of the Peripatetic school; author of a number of extant works such as *On Plants, On Stones, On First Principles*.

Thibaudet, Albert (1874–1936). Literary critic and political philosopher at the University of Geneva; student of Henri Bergson; author of *La république des professeurs* (1927) and *Les idées politiques de la France* (1932).

Tieck, Johann Ludwig (1773–1853). Poet and novelist; early figure in German Romanticism; author of the fairy tale *Der blonde Eckbert*.

Vigny, Alfred de (1797–1863). French Romantic poet and novelist; friend of Victor Hugo and member of the Académie française.

Villiers de l'Isle-Adam, Auguste (1838–1889). French Symbolist and horror writer.

APPENDIX 2

Books by Jean Wahl in English

A year in brackets identifies the year of publication of an original French edition.

1925 [1920]. *The Pluralist Philosophies of England and America.* Translated by Fred Rothwell. London: Open Court.

This book was originally Wahl's main doctoral thesis at the Sorbonne. It argues that "pluralism," the view that reality is an irreducible multiplicity, legitimating a diversity of approaches, reached its apex in nineteenth-century American philosophy, especially in William James, whose thought the majority of the text is given over to explicating. It was published simultaneously with his (then obligatory) "complementary thesis" *Le rôle de l'idée de l'instant dans la philosophie de Descartes*, an interpretation of Descartes that evinces the strong influence of his teacher, Henri Bergson. Both of these texts have recently been re-edited and republished in French, with introductions by contemporary philosophers.

1948. *The Philosopher's Way.* New York: Oxford University Press.

Written during Wahl's exile in the United States and originally published in English, this book is driven by the conviction that the twentieth century is seeing a radical transformation in how philosophy approaches its perennial questions. In numerous brief chapters, Wahl elucidates and analyzes the Western tradition's main theses about the basic concepts of metaphysics from the vantage that philosophy develops precisely through revolutionary changes—a conception traceable, perhaps, to Bachelard's influential thesis about "epistemological rup-tures" in scientific progress.

1949 [1949]. *A Short History of Existentialism.* Translated by Forrest Williams and Stanley Maron. New York: Philosophical Library.
Under sixty pages, this little book examines the thought of Kierkegaard, Jaspers/Heidegger, and Sartre and then offers a critique of existentialism. It is followed by a "discussion" of existentialism by Berdyaev, Koyré, Levinas, Marcel, and others. It was originally deliv-ered as a lecture in Paris in 1946.

1969 [1959]. *Philosophies of Existence: Introduction to the Basic Thought of Kierkegaard, Heidegger, Jaspers, Marcel, and Sartre.* Trans-lated by F. M. Lory. New York: Schocken Books.
This text is concerned, simply, with the fundamental categories common to the thought of the thinkers mentioned in the title, under-stood as opening a new and crucial chapter in the history of philoso-phy, expressing the heart of philosophy since Socrates, who "refused to separate his thought from his life" (vii). "It is hoped that a study of these categories . . . will lead the reader to reflect on his own existence. It is hoped, too, that he will see in these philosophies . . . primarily a call to his own subjectivity and perhaps the transition towards a new mode of thought that will combine sharpened subjectivity with a deep sense of communion with others and the world" (from the foreword, vii).

1974. *Voices in the Dark: Fifteen Poems of the Prison and the Camp.* Translated by Charles Guenther. Kirkwood, MO: The Printery.
These poems, as the title indicates, were composed while Wahl was being held by the Nazis and French collaborators at La Santé and then Drancy in 1941. It is a selection from the some one hundred poems he wrote during this time. A collector's item, the book is a limited edition run (120 copies) on handmade paper, and signed by the translator.